The

12

GEMSTONES

of

REVELATION

The 12 GEMSTONES of REVELATION

Unlocking the Significance of the Gemstone Phenomenon

MARY TRASK

DESTINY IMAGE® PUBLISHERS, INC.

P.O. Box 310, Shippensburg, PA 17257-0310

"Speaking to the Purposes of God for This Generation and for the Generations to Come."

This book and all other Destiny Image, Revival Press, MercyPlace, Fresh Bread, Destiny Image Fiction, and Treasure House books are available at Christian bookstores and distributors worldwide.

For a U.S. bookstore nearest you, call 1-800-722-6774.
For more information on foreign distributors, call 717-532-3040.
Or reach us on the Internet: www.destinyimage.com

ISBN 10: 0-7684-3105-0
ISBN 13: 978-0-7684-3105-6

For Worldwide Distribution, Printed in the U.S.A.
1 2 3 4 5 6 7 8 9 10 11 / 13 12 11 10 09

Dedication

This book is dedicated to my wonderful husband John, who has stood with me throughout the ups and downs of my faith walk as we venture toward the spiritual maturity both of us desire.

Acknowledgments

I would like to thank all my wonderful friends who proofread early versions of this book and encouraged me to follow through with this project. Your help was invaluable to me!

Endorsements

Mary's book reveals that we are the gems meant to lean against the chest of Jesus (as did Aaron's breastplate) and rest securely in His love. Her revelation of the meaning of Aaron's stones is amazing. You will be blessed as you read.

Julia Loren
Author, *Shifting Shadows of Supernatural Power* and
Shifting Shadows of Supernatural Experiences

I love it when the Lord manifests His presence. He often catches us by surprise and manifests tokens of His heavenly Kingdom in our midst; we call these tokens signs and wonders. Over the last decade or so, we have often witnessed the appearance of various types and sizes of gemstones during worship services. We also have interviewed many who have had such signs appear in their homes and places of business. What is this all about? What does it mean? The Lord often invites us into deeper intimacy with Him by perplexing us with wonders that provoke us to inquire of Him in the secret place. Every sign and wonder has a message from His heart. What do the gemstones mean? What is God saying? You will discover some profound revelation as you read Mary Trask's book, *The 12 Gemstones of Revelation*. And consider this: The Lord confirms His Word with signs following...hmmm? Read, ponder, and see what follows.

Patricia King
XPmedia.com

As a Christian counselor and therapist, I have attempted to remain a stable and conservative instrument in God's hands to touch people's lives. Mary Trask's awesome book, *The 12 Gemstones of Revelation*, has invited me to consider and embrace a different kind of manifestation of God. Not only does Mary clearly document with Scripture the symbolism of each stone, she also opens the door to a deeper understanding of the mysteries of God. Each person who reads this masterpiece with an open heart will experience how God encourages His people and makes His promises tangible. Fascinating, inspiring, and anointed!

Dr. Neecie Moore
CEO, Eagle Shield East

The Word of God is packed with hidden treasures. At first glance or with a casual read, one won't usually find them, but they are there, just under the surface waiting to be discovered and enjoyed. The problem is most of us don't take the time to find them. I suppose many of us don't know how to. Mary Trask helps us do just that. She helps us dig a little deeper to examine what on the surface seems to be just a lovely description of the wall in Revelation 21:19, and helps us see the greater meaning in each precious stone. She also reminds us that nothing is trivial in the Word of God. Who knows, maybe you will find a treasure of your own!

Kurt Snyder
Pastor, Destiny City Church
Tacoma, Washington

Table of Contents

Introduction

There is nothing random about our God, the Creator of Heaven and earth.

From the beginning of time, He has shown a special interest in His most beloved creation, man. Made in the image of God, man simply brought pleasure to the Creator.

God took great joy in placing man—formed with intricacies of thought and free will—in a world where thriving vegetation, celestial bodies, animal life of every variety, and even the stones themselves made known the character of God in an ongoing revelation. God knew the natural curiosities of man would lead to discovery after discovery. Like pieces in a puzzle, they all point to the Creator of Heaven and earth, causing man to stand in awe of his indescribable God and His amazing love.

Proverbs 25:2 tells us that it is the glory of God to conceal something, but it is the glory of kings to search it out. In other words, hidden truths have been strategically placed and are awaiting discovery—with all of them pointing back to the Creator. It is my belief that each discovery allows glimpses of understanding and further revelation into God's Kingdom.

If this is true, the beautiful precious stones described in the foundation of the wall surrounding New Jerusalem and those uncovered on earth are included in this principle (see Rev. 21:19-20). Though some question to which modern-day gemstone varieties the apostle John was referring in his vision (and how they correlate to the stones assigned to the 12 tribes of Israel), it is interesting to explore how one might interpret suggested symbolisms in relation to our Christian walk.

My initial interest in stones and beads went only as far as what I could purchase ready-made in the stores. However, when a favorite necklace broke, I visited a bead store so I could buy what I needed to repair the necklace myself. Walking in, I discovered a world full of amazing stones, each with its own unique pattern and color.

I made no effort to hurry while examining these God-created masterpieces. Old Testament verses came to mind describing stone altars used to memorialize encounters with God (for example, see Gen. 12:7; Josh. 8:30). In the New Testament, Romans 1:20 tells us that creation helps us better understand the attributes of God. Jesus Himself told the Pharisees that the stones themselves would cry out praises to God if the people did not worship Him (see Luke 19:40).

My curiosity was piqued.

What I've learned has both surprised and inspired me as I have created jewelry featuring each of the 12 stones mentioned in Revelation 21 and assigned to the 12 tribes. As I wear these pieces, the biblical principles and related promises of God represented by the stones encourage me greatly. It is my hope that you will be similarly inspired as we walk through a study of the promises and blessings of God as represented by His stones.

Chapter One
Walls of Salvation

G lenn, a middle-aged business man, sat before his home computer taking care of some necessary work related to his accounting business in the Seattle, Washington, area. Suddenly, he sensed the presence of the Lord in his office. He stopped what he was working on and began freely worshiping the Lord with childlike abandon. In the midst of his worship, Glenn heard something drop to the floor, so he stopped to investigate. Directly outside of his office door, he peered down to discover three walnut-sized, precision-cut gemstones sitting on the floor. One of the gemstones appeared to be a purple amethyst.[1]

Glenn was greatly blessed by his discovery, but this was not the first time this had happened.

Meanwhile, in Redding, California, young David and his wife Taylor had just returned from a prayer meeting where small, perfectly-cut diamonds had been found in the carpet of the home where they and others had gathered to pray. Later that same night, as they prepared for bed, they pulled back the covers to find a large, heart-shaped diamond resting atop the middle of their mattress. Curious, they brought the large diamond to a gemologist for examination. After studying the flawless stone, he promptly offered them $10,000 for the diamond.[2]

They refused to sell.

Reports of gemstones suddenly appearing at random locations both inside and outside the United States while faithful worshipers bask in the presence of God have brought many questions to the minds of believers. Why is this happening? Why have these supernatural gemstones been manifesting during the last several years? What is their significance?

While, for some, the answer might be found in the words of Psalms 115:3 which says, *"But our God is in heaven; He does whatever He pleases"*; others, such as myself, wonder what specific message the Lord might be trying to communicate to the Body of Christ through these gemstones.

CREATION SPEAKS

We are told in Romans 1:20 that all of creation offers us glimpses of our invisible God and His character. If this is true, then even gemstones (whether of earthly or heavenly origin) should point us to a better understanding of our amazing Creator.

To understand the message of these stones, we can look to Revelation 21:19-20 where 12 specific stones are mentioned in numerical order. These stones are described as adorning the foundation for the great wall surrounding New Jerusalem. By examining their numeric symbolisms, the original Greek and Hebrew meanings of the stones, and their probable assignments to each of the 12 tribes of Israel, we can establish some degree of understanding as to what some of these stones might signify.

We can similarly examine the meaning of the stones found by people like the couple in Redding. For example, since this couple found the heart-shaped diamond in their bed, it might signify the Lord's love for their intimacy with Him. We can add to our understanding by also considering the position of diamonds (or chrysolite) in the wall. As the seventh layer of the foundation stones and a stone likely assigned to the tribe of Naphtali, we will learn that diamonds (or chrysolite) represent great clarity in the Spirit for those who willingly empty themselves in humility to better chase after the affections of the Lord. (This will be further elaborated upon in Chapter Eight.)

The large purple stone discovered by the Seattle businessman might serve as a reminder of the twelfth and final stage of our sanctification process as represented by the amethyst. A stone often associated with the tribe of Issachar, I refer to it as God's "dream stone" representing fulfillment of all God has dreamed for us from the very moment of our conception. With Issachar's name meaning "our reward is with us," it's easy to see amethyst as representing all the joys that await the overcomers of this world.

One might wonder why God is choosing to shower heavenly gemstones upon certain individuals within His Church and what the stones might mean to the recipients. A woman I spoke to about this simply stated she felt the Lord was romancing her. When asked how her relationship with the Lord had changed since receiving the gemstones, she said she now experienced the Lord's love in a deeper way than before.

"This kind of stuff changes you!" she stated emphatically.

When asking Glenn why he thought he was chosen by God as a recipient of heavenly gemstones, he responded with a question in return: "Why not?"

When the gemstones first began appearing, he had struggled with thoughts of his own unworthiness. He felt there were many others who had been more faithful than himself. The fallacy of this kind of thinking was clearly exposed when a young woman confronted him with truth.

"Why not you?" she asked him.

Like many of us, Glenn needed a reminder that neither God's grace nor His favor are showered upon us because we've earned them. The gemstones, just like God's other gifts, are given according to His timetable and to the individuals of His choosing.

FILLED WITH HIS LOVE

Psalms 81:10 says, *"I am the Lord your God, who brought you out of the land of Egypt; open your mouth wide, and I will fill it."* In his book *The Treasury of David*, Charles Spurgeon indicates that an ancient custom of Persian kings was to invite honored guests (usually ambassadors) to open wide their mouths so the king could cram them with sweetmeats. If he was particularly pleased with an individual, jewels would sometimes be included in the mouthful.[3]

As we apply this same principle to our own lives, we see it is the King of kings choice which of His amazing treasures He desires to place within the mouths of His beloved children. Our task is only to *open wide our mouths* in hunger for more, like famished chicks, to receive everything with which He chooses to bless us.

As this debris of Heaven continues to fall, it might behoove us to look more carefully at the wall itself, so we might better understand what these stones represent. Isaiah 26:1 says, *"... God will appoint salvation for walls and bulwarks."* Isaiah 60:18 states that *"... you shall call your walls Salvation, and your gates Praise."* Isaiah 54:11-12 describes our foundations and walls as being adorned with *"colorful gems"* and *"precious stones."*

By putting all of these references together, we see that the wall and its foundations described in Revelation 21 are illustrations of the amazing wall of salvation, with New Jerusalem representing the Church as the Bride of Christ. In understanding the symbolism of the stones in the wall, we can all better appreciate this incredible gift of God—something we call salvation.

In studying God's Word, it is important to remember that there are many different facets and levels of learning that each of us can achieve while growing in intimacy with our Lord. I acknowledge that the truths presented here are only one way one might interpret the stones and walls of salvation. Undoubtedly, others will see the same things in a different light and come to equally valid conclusions.

First Corinthians 13:12 says we all see in part and understand in part, but by offering this study of the stones from a new perspective, it is my hope to challenge and inspire each of us to continue our pursuit of the Lover of our souls.

Together, we can take the time to examine each of the 12 stones listed in Revelation 21 while exploring their spiritual significance and the manner in which each might represent another facet in this gift of salvation. The stories and testimonies to follow will, I'm sure, both challenge and inspire you, as they have me.

ENDNOTES

1. Confirmed via phone interview, and I have seen the stone myself. It appears to be an amethyst.

2. Bill Johnson, Sermon: "The Climate for Increasing Faith," Bethel Church, Redding, CA January 27, 2008.

3. Charles H. Spurgeon, "Commentary on Psalms 81:10." "The Treasury of David." <http://bible.crosswalk.com/Commentaries/Treasuryof David/tod.cgi?book=ps&chapter=081&verse=010>. 1865-1885 (accessed April 29, 2009).

Chapter Two
Who Am I... Really?

JASPER—BENJAMIN'S STONE

The ground glistened in the morning sunlight after an overnight spring rain brought much-needed moisture to the area. A lone figure dressed in a blue fur-collared coat and matching hat scurried down the sidewalk toward school.

The year was 1961 and she was late.

Living only blocks from the school, the nearly six-year-old felt very capable of walking herself to class that morning. Mom was busy with her younger siblings and the child had only one major street to cross.

The student crossing guards had already abandoned their posts when she arrived at the busy street. The young girl stood timidly on the curb with the crosswalk in front of her awaiting her opportunity to go. A car in the far lane, seeing her dilemma, pulled to a stop. The woman driver motioned for the child to cross the street while she waited.

The parked car that blocked the young girl's view to the left didn't concern her. An adult told her to go so, trustingly, she stepped off the curb and into the crosswalk. Just barely beyond the parked car, the sound of squealing brakes and tires sliding on slick asphalt caused the child to turn and look into the shiny grill of an approaching car; it was only moments before impact.

Then everything went black.

Her small body was tossed into the air like a rag doll and landed in a heap in the middle of the crosswalk. Blood poured out upon the asphalt and soaked into her coat turning it a deep shade of purple. In a panic, sickened adults gathered around the limp figure awaiting transportation to the nearest hospital.

"Two broken ribs and undetermined internal injuries," was the verdict finally given to the girl's grief-stricken parents. "There's nothing you can do but go home and pray," they were told. They called everyone they knew and prayers began to go up on behalf of the child.

Meanwhile, feeling warm and secure, the child waited in darkness. A strangely familiar voice spoke to her and told her two important things for the days that followed. First, she would be fine; second, when she grew up, she would work for Him.

That evening, the child awoke suddenly from her comatose state and sat up to better inspect the sterile hospital room in which she found herself. A passing nurse happened to see the child moving and immediately summoned the doctor. Finding the girl in no apparent pain during his examination, he ordered a new set of x-rays to be taken immediately.

The new x-rays showed no broken bones at all!

After three days, the child was released to go home with nothing more than some stitches on the side of her head and a little weakness that soon subsided. Realizing her life had been spared for a reason, the girl often wondered about God while growing up. She attended church each Sunday with her family and heard all the stories about Jesus. The girl secretly wished that she could have been alive in Bible times to meet Jesus in person.

I was that girl. Nine long years would pass before my deepest desire came true. I finally met Jesus, and as He washed away the years of sin that had hardened my heart, I found the peace for which I had been searching.

This transformation established the foundation from which my faith could grow. Many more years sailed by before I came to appreciate the wonderful message God left for us in Revelation 21—the message describing the brilliant gemstone wall surrounding New Jerusalem in Heaven.

*The foundations of the wall of the city were adorned with all kinds of precious stones: the first foundation was **jasper...** (Revelation 21:19).*

John the apostle attempted to describe the visionary scenes that flashed before him during his imprisonment on the island of Patmos somewhere between the years A.D. 70 and A.D. 95. His vision included great details of things befalling the earth in the last days, climaxing with a descent of the New Jerusalem from Heaven onto the earth.

Laid within the New Jerusalem's walls and foundations, he saw a variety of precious stones and gems flashing in indescribable hues; he recounted the vision for us in the Book of Revelation.

THE FIRST FOUNDATION

One stone mentioned several times in this account is jasper. John says the city itself glowed with the glory of God, "like a jasper stone, clear as crystal" (Rev. 21:11). The walls of the city were composed of clear jasper and adorned with a multitude of precious stones. The 12 gates were pearls and the streets were transparent gold like glass (see Rev. 21:18-21). Obviously the stones and gold found in Heaven are quite different from what we see here on earth.

Colossians 2:17, Hebrews 8:5, and Hebrews 10:1 tell us that the things we see on earth are mere shadows of what is in Heaven. Could the varieties of stones we now see on earth be only "shadow versions" of heavenly stones? Precious stones and gold, when completely saturated with the glory of God, might have a completely different appearance.

In considering jasper, the first stone mentioned in the foundation of the amazing wall of gemstones, we find some experts in agreement that jasper was most likely assigned to the tribe of Benjamin.[1]

One can imagine the Benjamites pointing out the jasper set into the high priest's breastplate, along with the other 11 stones. What they didn't realize is that jasper represented far more than their small tribe. Jasper represented adoption, future transformation, rebirth as Heaven's royalty, and the highly favored children of the Eternal King.[2] This is the first of 12 stones whose unique messages can completely alter our way of thinking and living.

The promises given to Benjamin were established even at his birth. Rachel, who died delivering him, wanted to name him "son of my sorrow." Jacob intervened and instead established him as a favored son (see Gen. 35:18).

We see in Psalms 68:27 and other places in the Bible that the Benjamites saw themselves as small and inferior to the other eleven tribes. However, in Genesis 49:27 Jacob declared Benjamin to be a ravenous wolf that establishes his rightful authority. Later in Deuteronomy 33:12, Moses referred to Benjamin as *"beloved of the Lord"* one who *"shall dwell in safety between His shoulders."* Isn't this a beautiful picture of the good Shepherd of Psalm 23?

Today, jasper can be found in a smorgasbord of colors and patterns, but is usually red, brown, gold, or green. Modern varieties of jasper are generally named according to the pattern found within their colorful bands of chalcedony, microcrystalline quartz, and other minerals.[3] One popular variety of the stone is "landscape jasper" which appears to capture small snapshots of nature within its varied markings and swirls of color.

Historically, jasper was valued as a gemstone, but was also used for seals, signets, and small figurines. Some early ancestors believed jasper could prevent sorrow, protect the owner from drowning, and even ward off droughts. In ancient Rome, prior to a young woman's marriage, her father would give her a ring with the family seal engraved in jasper. This ring not only demonstrated the father's affection for his daughter, but was also used as a seal for wine jars and food containers. With this seal in place, these containers could only be opened by the new mistress of the house.

In Hebrew we find the word *jasper* meaning "to polish."[4] With its assignment as the first foundation stone for the New Jerusalem and the stone of the tribe of Benjamin, we can further understand it to represent "the beginning," recognizing God as the Source of all and recognizing our position as the "son of the right hand," meaning a favored son or daughter.

When putting all this together, we can understand jasper and this beginning stage of our developing relationship with the Lord as the first baby steps of salvation. We see our own sinfulness before God, yet by agreeing with Him and receiving His gift of forgiveness, our lives are transformed. This new lifestyle before us prepares us for the great authority we will learn to use as favored children of God's Kingdom. This beginning stage is played out for us in John 4:1-30 when Jesus went into the land of Samaria and met with a desperate woman at the well.

In this encounter, Jesus made it very clear to the Samaritan woman that her own resources would never truly fill the spiritual need she had. She was a sinner who needed to admit her sins so she could be released from her guilt through the forgiveness offered by Jesus. Everything *secret* was exposed before God. Nothing was hidden and she had nothing to say in denial. Her need for Him and the living water He offered was made crystal clear.

Though Jesus recognized her sin, He offered her a chance to be released from the guilt simply by responding to the call He made to her heart. Suddenly the woman understood and took off running into the town yelling as she went, *"Come, see a Man who told me all things that I ever did. Could this be the Christ?"* (John 4:29).

She was a changed woman and no longer held back by the shame of her adulterous affairs. Jesus had revealed the failures of her life, but offered love and forgiveness in exchange for her guilt. The woman jumped at the chance to be free and immediately became a bold witness for the Messiah.

Because of her true repentance and humility before God, the woman at the well was able to make that "impossible" leap of faith to become a daughter of the Kingdom. Her guilt was gone and she was now a "new creation in Christ." Though she had much to learn about the Kingdom of God, the message of Jesus reached her broken heart and transformed her.

I believe the message Jesus brought her was threefold:

1. I am the Messiah offering you all you lack.
2. I know all about you and your failures, and I still love you.
3. I'm inviting you to receive the love I offer.

The woman's response to His invitation was also threefold:

1. I believe who You are.
2. I acknowledge my sin.
3. I accept Your offer of love and forgiveness.

So radical was this woman's surrender to the deep probing of Jesus that she felt compelled to announce to the entire village that she had met the Messiah.

My New Beginning

My own introduction to the Kingdom of God was somewhat similar to the woman at the well. Though not involved in adulterous affairs as the Samaritan woman was, darkness plagued my life. At 15, I found myself fighting fears, depression, jealousy, insecurity, and anger. Though appearing well enough on the outside, inwardly I was miserable and looking for something more.

Having read David Wilkerson's book *The Cross and the Switchblade* only a short time before, my spiritual hunger for real evidence of a living and powerful God was at an all-time high. I was sick of religious form that only focused on outward appearances. Even at 15 years of age, I could see that "good behavior" was never good enough to bring real joy;

and religious activities did little to display life-changing power as demonstrated for us in the Bible.

Even while searching my heart for answers, my parents heard reports of healing miracles occurring at a local prayer meeting. They began attending and each week brought back stories of instantaneous healings. Finally, my curiosity got the best of me and I asked if I could attend the next meeting with them.

Not knowing what to expect, I tried to slip in unnoticed by the group in hopes of acting as only an observer. Instead, I was overwhelmed by a sense of unconditional love that filled the room. I sat nervously on the outside of the group waiting for the miracles to occur. Simple songs of heartfelt praise and worship flowed out of the participants while spontaneous prayers erupted from individuals as they sat before God.

Both the songs and prayers impressed me.

Men and women closed their eyes; they lifted their hands worshiping and praying as if Jesus were actually in their midst. That intrigued me! I had never seen such passion before. Though no physical miracles occurred that evening, my heart had been touched by their overflowing love. So I decided to try it again the following week.

When that night finally arrived, instead of just watching everyone as I had the previous week, I thought that if I attempted to pray like those around me, my heart might become just as impassioned as theirs. However, by the end of the meeting, I was still depressed and as miserable as before.

Nothing had changed.

Feeling awkward and out of place, I tried covering up my insecurities by speaking with one of the young men attending the meeting. We had spoken only briefly when he suddenly stopped mid-sentence and asked if I had ever given my life to the Lord. His question stunned me.

"I was raised in church," I countered defensively.

"But have you ever invited Jesus to be in control of your life?" he pressed on.

"No, I guess not."

"Well, how about tonight... right now?"

Because of my Christian education and regular church attendance, I assumed I was already a Christian. Verbally inviting Jesus into my life seemed like such a trite thing to do, but it couldn't possibly hurt anything, I reasoned, so why not do it?

After being led into another room, I sat in a chair while several others gathered around me for prayer. My friend led me in a simple prayer inviting Jesus into my life. Though the prayer was basic, I was genuine in my surrender to God. My miserable life was His and He could do whatever He wanted with it.

The prayers of the surrounding saints went up like incense before God as they cried out on my behalf. Suddenly the sound of their prayers changed from English to a language I couldn't understand.

It must be Latin or something, I reasoned; but my logical analysis was short-lived. Something was stirring within me.

In a brief moment of time, I was surrounded by a great light and found myself in the presence of God. Without an exchange of words, I suddenly knew that I was in the presence of the almighty, all powerful, Creator of the universe! This revelation literally shook me to my core... and there I stood feeling very exposed and fearful in His presence. My sinfulness and unworthiness were very evident, but before I had a chance to draw back in fear, I was encompassed by a blanket of His love; it permeated every part of my being.

It was more than I could comprehend! Why me? How could He love someone as insignificant as me? And still the waves of His love continued washing over me as I wept tears of joy that brought great healing to my soul.

In the midst of all this, a voice instructed me to open my mouth to allow the power of God to flow freely. I don't know if the voice was of human or supernatural origin, but I knew I needed to obey, so I opened my mouth and a heavenly language literally gushed out of me like water rushing out of an opened dam.

The experience was so beyond my human emotions, I found myself laughing one moment and crying the next. Waves of God's power surged through my body. I couldn't stop speaking in this heavenly language; nor did I want to! It was all so wonderful! I now knew without a shadow of a doubt that Jesus was alive and well—and His Holy Spirit was residing in me!

After hours of being unable to move out of that chair, I finally gained enough strength to get up and move on my own. I felt light and giddy as though a million pounds had been lifted off my back. Indescribable joy filled me to overflowing and the first thing I wanted to do was to tell my older brother about the wonderful thing Jesus had done for me. Several days later, back at school, I was compelled to tell every person I saw that that Jesus was real!

"Come to the next prayer meeting with me!" I coaxed them. "You can meet Him for yourself."

My response to the revelation of Jesus was much like that of the Samaritan woman at the well. Both of us had been slaves to sin. The piercing gaze of our God revealed our need and spiritual desperation. Sin's exposure broke down any tinge of self-righteousness. The forgiving love of the Savior removed the shame and replaced it with a spirit of adoption into His Kingdom.

Jasper, the first foundation stone, serves as a reminder of this incredible exchange. By acknowledging our sin before Him and accepting His sacrifice, we receive Jesus' payment for our sin, thereby opening the way for us to become favored children of God.

It is easy to see why God desires to communicate His love and His purposes to us; He does so through many means. These glimpses of nature captured in jasper can help us to recall our first steps in God's adoption process. Jesus' death on the cross paid the price for each of us, that we might live a life worthy of His high calling. Jasper can be a symbol of our own humble beginnings and can represent both a wall of protection and the solid foundation which allows us to stand before God. As wonderful as this promise is, this is only the first of 12 incredible promises from God.

What precious treasure jasper can be as we look at it as a reminder of our own adoption as favored sons and daughters in the Kingdom of God!

REFLECTIONS ON THE ROCK

If you're not absolutely certain that you are a favored son or daughter within God's Kingdom, there is a way to change that. Romans 3:23 tells us our sin has caused separation between us and God. Without Jesus and the sacrifice He made on the cross, we would have absolutely no hope of ever getting to Heaven when we die. By confessing our sins to God, we are admitting our need for the blood of Jesus to wash away our guilt.

Once we have agreed with God, we have the great privilege of inviting Jesus to live within us. When this occurs, radical changes take place. Not only does the burden of sin lift off us, but we are also able to freely experience the love the Father has had for us from the beginning.

This outpouring of love descends upon us in many ways. If we continue our pursuit for more in the Kingdom of God, we will begin to experience His supernatural joy and the peace that passes all understanding within our lives (see Phil. 4:7).

I encourage you to make your declaration of faith and move into all God has planned for your life. You won't regret this important eternal decision!

LET'S PRAY!

Lord Jesus, I openly declare that You are the perfect Son of God sent to earth to suffer and die a horrible death so I can be forgiven of my sins. I acknowledge my many sins and failures before You and humbly ask for Your forgiveness. I ask that in Your mercy You would wash me in the blood of Your sacrifice that I might become pure in God's eyes.

In the name of Jesus, I now command any spirits of darkness holding me captive to leave me now! I send you to the feet of Jesus! I don't want you any more! Go now! You are no longer welcome in my life!

Father God, I now ask that You would fill me with Your Holy Spirit and power that I might move forward in Your grace. Grant me all that I need to become the person You have designed me to be. Please send godly people into my path who might encourage and further instruct me as I move ahead with You. I ask all this in Jesus' name. Amen.

THE LORD'S WORD TO YOU

Dear favored child,

When you look at jasper, I want you to no longer believe the lie of insignificance, especially in My Kingdom. You've been adopted. I paid a great price for you. You are very precious and as My child, you have been endued with My authority. Follow Me on this path of preparation that I may teach you how to walk as I did on this earth. Will you trust Me as we walk together toward maturity?

ENDNOTES

1. John Gill, Commentary *John Gill's Exposition of the Bible.* <http://bible.crosswalk.com/Commentaries/GillsExposition oftheBible/, 1999, (accessed April 29, 2009).

2. International Colored Gemstone Association. "Lapis Lazuli." http://www.gemstone.org/gem-by-gem/english/lapis.html (accessed April 29, 2009).

3. Ibid. "Jasper: Landscape in Stone." http://www.gemstone
   .org/gem-by-gem/english/jasper.html (accessed April 29,
   2009).

4. *The New Strong's Exhaustive Numbers and Concordance with
   Expanded Greek-Hebrew Dictionary.* CD-ROM. Biblesoft, Inc.,
   and International Bible Translators, Inc., s.v. "yashepheh," (OT
   3471).

Chapter Three

The Dawning of Two Realms

LAPIS LAZULI/SAPPHIRE—DAN'S STONE

...Behold, I will lay your stones with colorful
gems and lay your foundations
*with **sapphires** (Isaiah 54:11).*

Several years ago, Delores, a grandmother and housewife living in the Puget Sound area of Washington State, was in her laundry room working when the voice of the Lord suddenly spoke to her heart.

"You are like a jewel to Me, tried and true...a sapphire. I'm proud of you," He said.

Greatly moved by this, Delores then asked the Holy Spirit to teach her about the stones in the Bible. In her study that week, the Holy Spirit directed her to specific passages throughout the Bible. She read in the Book of Exodus about the *"paved work of sapphire stone"* under God's feet as He met with Moses, the priests, and the 70 elders on His mountain (see Exod. 24:10).

In the Book of Ezekiel, she learned how the sapphire's brilliant blues flashed from under the throne of God (Ezek. 1:26). Delores came to understand that Jesus truly was the Rock of our salvation who endured great testing while on earth.

Both the spoken and written Word of God gave her great encouragement as she was enduring some challenging trials at that time. She clung to the words of Malachi 3:17 promising that we are as jewels before the Lord. Later, as she pondered all she had learned about sapphires, she realized that blue was her favorite color, something she wore all the time. That revelation just added to her interest in the stone.

One day in prayer, Delores asked the Lord for a sapphire ring so she could be reminded of all the encouragement He had spoken to her heart. She didn't want just a tiny little stone, however. She wanted a large sapphire with smaller stones set in a circle around it. At first, even her husband was not aware of her desire for a sapphire ring.

Later that summer, the couple's son was getting married and a dear friend, Jill, surprised Delores with a pair of diamond stud earrings to wear for the wedding. Unfortunately, she didn't have pierced ears, so she was forced to return the gift to her friend. When Jill learned of her error, she promptly offered Delores a choice between three different sapphire rings she had.

While looking at the three rings, Delores instantly knew which ring was the one for which she had prayed! The oval princess-cut sapphire was surrounded by a ring of smaller white sapphires on a silver band looking very much like a royal crown.

Today, the beautiful sapphire ring daily graces Delores's hand. Each time she looks at it, she is reminded of the precious promises given to her by the Lord Himself. With this physical manifestation of the Lord's love for her, this precious woman finds it much easier to believe in faith for other challenges she and her family face from time to time.

HISTORY OF THE BLUE STONES

Just as Delores found herself encouraged by the deep blue hues of the sapphire, we can imagine how the Danites must have felt as they watched their blue stone glisten in the sunlight next to the other eleven stones on the high priest's breastplate. Though just a stone, it must have been inspiring to think that God had selected that particular stone to represent their tribe. They could be confident that God remembered each of them; and as a symbol of His love, He left instructions for the high priest to wear the breastplate with the gemstone close to his heart.[1]

Often translated as "sapphire" in both Greek and Hebrew, *lapis lazuli* (or *lazurite*) was most likely the blue stone found in the breastplate of the high priest, assigned to the tribe of Dan and described as the second foundation stone in the New Jerusalem. It was also reportedly one of the first stones ever used and worn for jewelry. History indicates that the ancient city of Ur, the original home of Abraham and Lot, traded this beautiful stone for thousands of years.[2]

In the world of art, artists known as the Old Masters would actually pulverize lapis lazuli, add it to a mixture of binding agents, and use it as bright blue paint for their watercolors, tempera, and oil paintings. Consequently, the brilliant blues shown in many of the old world masterpieces have retained their color for hundreds of years.

BIBLICAL SIGNIFICANCE OF THE BLUE STONES

From a biblical standpoint, the selection of lapis as the second foundation stone is significant. The number *two* represents division or separation. The name *Dan* is defined in the Hebrew as "dawn, to judge, to rule". The word *sapphire* represents "scratching, to score, inscribe, enumerate, recount, celebrate, declare, and a reckoning."[3]

When we put all of these together, we can see that the dawning of Truth (Jesus) has brought a distinct call for separation from the darkness of this world. We have been marked by the love of the Father and are in the beginning stages of learning what it means to allow God to rule and reign in our lives. Some have also come to understand the color *blue* as symbolizing the Spirit of Grace or Might working in our lives, while others see it as a symbol or reminder of Heaven and the authority we carry.

In studying the progression of the redemption/adoption process, we first see ourselves being loosed from the kingdom of darkness as we cry out to Jesus. His blood covers our sin and the chains of sin are loosed around us. However, Scriptures indicate that further freedom occurs as we learn to release others from their offenses against us (see Luke 11:4). Luke 6:37 tells us, *"Forgive and you will be forgiven."*

This whole forgiving process is related to grace and can be described as a kind of departing from or even divorcing the old offenses.[4] If we accept God's call to forgive and release others, we ourselves will be able to move into the position of being fully forgiven. As we make our choices to forgive, we learn that the word *forgiveness* in Ephesians 1:7 indicates that if we forgive, then the offenses will have no more effect upon us. By this, we can also understand the impact of offenses upon us if we continue to hold on to them.

It is during this sapphire or second level of growth that we are called upon to separate ourselves from the destructive forces of sin so we can continue pressing into maturity in the Kingdom of God.

As sapphire (or lapis lazuli) is considered to be Dan's stone, it's important to examine the prophetic promises given to Dan so that we may apply these same promises to our own lives as we progress forward. We see in Genesis 49:16 that Jacob declared Dan to be a judge over his people. He follows this statement by describing Dan's authority as similar to a serpent taking down a rider by attacking the horse. Later Moses described Dan as a lion's whelp or cub (see Deut. 33:22).

Both of these prophetic pictures clearly lay out the battles we must embark upon in order to be fully free from our past. Past lies, past offenses, and past injustices must be identified and dealt with in prayer in order for us to experience the joys of greater spiritual freedom in our lives.

At this stage of maturity, the lion's cub is a novice; therefore, these verses indicate the wisdom in first attacking the method by which sin enters (the horse) rather than engaging direct confrontation (with the rider). By separating ourselves from areas of darkness or temptations of our past, we will have the opportunity to strengthen this new way of living with less enticement to fall back into our old patterns of life.

Walking in a continual state of blessing and forgiveness will help us strengthen the work of God within our hearts. If we're tempted to entertain thoughts of unforgiveness, bitterness, jealousy, envy, and judgment, we are putting ourselves back into that former state of sin. We don't forgive, so we can't be forgiven of our offenses! This is the time the Holy Spirit wants to focus on our "stinkin' thinkin'" so we can learn how to focus on the things of the Spirit and not the things of the flesh.

ABRAM AND THE BLUE STONES

The brilliant blues of sapphires and lapis lazuli and the separation process they represent might remind us of some key events in the life of Abram that appear to parallel this second stage in the life of a believer. The first of Abram's separation process was actually initiated by Terah, his father, who led his family out of Ur of the Chaldees to the northern city of Haran as told in Genesis 11:31. We don't know what caused Terah to leave the well-developed city of Ur. Archeological findings in this southern Mesopotamian region have found that the citizens of Ur were highly educated and their commerce was booming.[5] At the same time, however, idolatry was also very prominent within the households of Ur; this may have been a motivating factor in Terah's move.

In Genesis 12:1-3, we find the Lord urging Abram to get out from his country, his family, and his father's house in order to find the land that God had for him. This move would be involved in Abram's being both blessed and a blessing to all the families of the earth. Although Haran was a step in the right direction, further separation was needed; the Lord called Abram to leave it all behind in order to find the promised land.

In Luke 18:29-30 Jesus says:

Assuredly, I say to you, there is no one who has left house or parents or brothers or wife or children, for the sake of the kingdom of God, who shall not receive many times more in this present time, and in the age to come eternal life.

Just as Abram had to walk away from all he knew, so we are called to leave behind the familiar and comfortable surroundings for which our flesh constantly cries out. Why? In order to see the fulfillment of the greater promise God offers to those who seek Him with their whole heart. God has great blessings in store for those who truly love Him, but we must be diligent in searching our own hearts to make sure we have not allowed our comfort to be the determining factor in our life decisions.

As we watch the life of Abram, we see his inner transformation slowly take place as he grows to become the father of our faith. Abram, the high or proud father, becomes Abraham, the father of many nations (see Gen. 17:5). His pride of self-sufficiency is broken as he takes his barren wife and young nephew to search after the plan of God for his life.

Later on, we see a need for further division—between Abraham and Lot—as their great wealth in cattle and their search for water began to put a strain upon the land. Lot chose the location that appeared better, while Abraham maintained his separation from the influences of the world at that time.

Lot ended with the finer piece of land, but it meant that he and his family would live in Sodom. The Bible tells us that righteous Lot was oppressed and tormented daily by the wickedness of those lawless individuals surrounding him (see 2 Pet. 2:7-8). What's puzzling is the fact that, although Lot was oppressed and grieved by the sin around him, he chose to remain in Sodom. He and his family had obviously grown accustomed to the comforts of civilization.

We see evidence of this when Lot and his family flee their home. As they ran, Lot's wife looked back to her old life with longing. Her willful disobedience to the angel's instructions resulted in her own destruction, even as the cities of Sodom and Gomorrah were decimated (see Gen. 19:26).

Even before Lot's departure from Sodom, we see him pleading with the angel to allow him to escape to Zoar, another city in the valley (see

Gen. 19:22). Lot asked this because he feared that some evil would overtake him and he would die (see Gen. 19:18-20).

After Lot arrived at Zoar, the destruction of the nearby cities and the loss of his wife shook him so badly that he ended up leaving Zoar and hiding with his daughters in a mountainside cave (see Gen. 19:30).

Lot and his daughters did survive because of Abraham's intercession for them, but what kind of message had Lot passed on to his daughters? Their close proximity and affiliation with the surrounding sin of Sodom had greatly influenced his girls. We see this in their obvious lack of godly conviction as they decided to get their father drunk so they could be impregnated by him. The two nations created by this act, Moab and Ammon, would be a thorn in the side of Israel throughout all of history; and their descendants still plague Israel to this day!

The life of Lot can present both a lesson and a warning for all of us. Lot *was* righteous, according to Second Peter 2:8; but it is apparent that his unwillingness to separate himself from the comforts of this life resulted in the loss of all he owned, the loss of his wife, and the corruption of his two daughters. One has to ask, *Was it worth it?*

Abraham, on the other hand, was a man who was willing to choose repeatedly whatever separation or division the Lord required of him along the pathway to spiritual growth. Whether it was circumcision or the command to sacrifice his only son, Abraham withheld nothing from God. As a result, the Lord was able to take this man and establish him as the father of our faith on this earth.

THE LIFE OF SEPARATION

The life of division and separation is a principle of faith that is repeated throughout the Bible. We're not talking about a negative division of the flesh occurring as a result of gossip, backbiting, jealousy, and the like. The division referred to here is separation from the darkness of this world so we can embrace the truth wholeheartedly. Love of this world is warring with the love of truth—and our choices today will make a difference for us later.

Jesus described this process in Matthew 7:13-14 when He said:

Enter by the narrow gate; for wide is the gate and broad is the way that leads to destruction, and there are many who go in by it. Because narrow is the gate and difficult is the way which leads to life, and there are few who find it.

These verses inform us that the way to fullness in the Kingdom of God is a narrow path. This path requires each of us to gradually lay aside all that would prevent us from entering. Difficult choices must be made to enter the promised land of the Spirit here on earth. Many of us strive against the Holy Spirit's probing into our hearts. Yet, He works to reveal the hidden thoughts and intentions of our sinful flesh (see Heb. 4:12).

I've had my tussles in this area as well. I'm always discovering new areas of sin that seem to pop up out of nowhere, especially in difficult situations. God's challenge first encourages me to admit my sin and then separate myself from it through His gift of repentance.

One early battle in this separation process occurred shortly after I became a Christian. After attending one of my daily summer classes in San Francisco, I had the usual 45-minute bus ride back to my East Bay area home. Several delays during that hot afternoon caused me to be one of the last passengers to board the bus. The only available seat was on the very last row right next to the restroom. Though not happy about the seating, I decided I had no alternative.

As the bus took off, weaving back and forth through traffic, my stomach began churning with motion sickness. All my concentration was focused on keeping my eyes glued to the road directly ahead as I tried in vain to ignore the waves of nausea. Once on the relatively straight highway, I was able to relax a little bit. Still, the packed bus and warm temperatures outside made the inside of the bus warm and stuffy—not good for an upset stomach.

As the steady drone of the engine continued, many of the passengers dozed off, including the rather portly gentleman sitting next to me. In fact, he was so comfortable that his head began shifting to one side—in my direction! As the bus rambled on, the weight of his body began crushing me further against the wall of the restroom.

I was trapped with no place to go!

In my teenage mind, I could not envision a worse scenario. All I could think about was the fact that I had to endure these very uncomfortable conditions for the rest of my trip home. I honestly didn't think I would survive. My misery was complete.

It was in the midst of all this that I suddenly heard a man's voice speaking to me. "Do you love Me?" He inquired.

My first reaction was to check the "sleeping giant" resting comfortably on my shoulder.

Was he trying to make a pass at me? I was horrified at the possibility! Thankfully, he was still sleeping, and apart from the fact that I was serving as his pillow, he was unaware of me. I waited for a moment and carefully scanned the occupants of the bus to see if they had heard the voice, too, but no one was looking in my direction. Puzzled, I dismissed the voice as a figment of my imagination and went back to my miseries.

"Do you love Me?" the voice asked again.

This time I was certain about what I had heard. Was someone playing a cruel trick on me or were they speaking to someone else? Determined to catch the culprit, I carefully scrutinized each passenger, but no one was making eye contact or even glancing in my direction.

Suddenly, I heard the voice again and realized who was speaking to me!

"Do you love Me?" the voice repeated.

In an instant, I was caught up into another realm where I was only aware of God's presence before me. My fears and insecurities rose up as His light surrounded me.

Why was He speaking to me? I wondered. I'm only a kid, not anyone *significant*. However, His probing question remained and I had to respond.

"Yes, Lord. I love You."

The words tumbled out awkwardly. I didn't *feel* as though I loved Him at that moment. Instead, I felt ashamed—as if my hand had been caught in a cookie jar.

"If you love Me, then I want you to thank Me," He instructed.

At first, His request puzzled me. *How do you thank Him when you're in the middle of terrible circumstances like this?* I wondered. His silence said it all. I knew what He wanted.

Suddenly I was back in the bus and once again aware of my surroundings. I really did love the Lord and *did* want to obey Him, so I took a breath and began quietly thanking Him for everything. And I mean *everything!*

My litany of thanksgiving started with the most obvious issue: my upset stomach. Though I didn't really mean it at the time, I stepped out in obedience. My next *gift* of thanksgiving focused on the crushing weight of my neighbor still pressing me as he snored contentedly. I thanked God for the sweltering heat and every other discomfort I was experiencing at the time.

From there, my focus began shifting into more positive areas. I thanked Him for my family and the friends with which He had blessed me. I thanked Him for my home, my room, my belongings. I expressed thankfulness for my relationship with Him and all He was teaching me. The list went on and on.

As words of praise and thanksgiving began flowing I noticed a huge change occurring inside me. In the beginning, my words felt mechanical, not genuine at all; but as I continued, I literally felt a river of joy bubbling up from within. Wave after wave of joy washed over me, and suddenly I lost all concern for my personal comfort and surroundings. I no longer felt sick and bothered by my neighbor; but instead, I had to try containing my joy in the Lord until I arrived home and was able to share it with my family.

When the bus finally came to my stop, I literally sprang from my seat and ran home.

"Mom! Guess what?" I shouted while pushing open the front door. "God spoke to me on the bus!"

At 16 years of age, I was able to learn from the Lord some valuable lessons through this experience. God, in His great wisdom, allowed these uncomfortable circumstances as an opportunity for me to grow. His continued love for me, in spite of my grumbling heart, surprised me. I understood that His love for me was not based on performance. He loves each of us with an unconditional love and calls us only to respond to His love.

Another lesson drawn from this experience was the idea that, through thankfulness and praise, I was given a way out of my miserable condition. When I placed my focus back on the Lord and off my circumstances, great joy flooded my heart, even though my circumstances hadn't changed. My heart was freed from grumbling and complaining; instead, it was lifted up into heavenly places.

EMBRACE THE SEPARATION PROCESS

Drawing back into our sin nature is a normal response to our natural circumstances. The Holy Spirit's job is to probe and convict us of sin so we can begin to understand the difference between walking in our human nature and walking in God's supernatural nature. We must learn to leave behind the old ways of thinking and responding so we can learn to live above our immediate circumstances.

Does this separation process offend our flesh and confound our logic? Absolutely! But embracing the correction of the Holy Spirit and responding to God's upward call will eventually bring us to a place of greater joy and freedom than previously imagined.

How wonderful to think that the beautiful blue hues found in lapis lazuli can remind us of the Holy Spirit's cutting edge—the line of division that separates us from the ways of the world so that we can gain entrance into His supernatural side of existence on this planet. Layer by layer, the things that seek to hinder us are revealed. Sapphire and lapis truly can be symbols of God's separation process as we choose the narrow path that leads to life.

REFLECTIONS ON THE ROCK

After reading this chapter you may feel that more separation is needed in your own life in order to fully embrace the direction God has for you. Let me pose some questions for your consideration.

Have you struggled with falling into old sin patterns and then felt condemned over your failures? Do you find yourself hanging out with the same friends, doing the same things that draw you back into the ways of the world? Are there offenses in your life that you haven't yet released? Are you able to actually pray and bless those who have wounded you or are you still holding a grudge?

This struggle between light and darkness is something with which we all battle at different times and in different ways, but if you recognize that you are deliberately allowing ungodly influences into your life, I encourage you to make some necessary changes so you don't find yourself overcome with darkness.

LET'S PRAY!

Lord Jesus, I come before You and ask, first of all, for Your forgiveness for disobeying the Holy Spirit's promptings to turn from sin and flee from temptations. Help me to totally forgive others who may have offended or even wounded me so I can be forgiven and released of my own offenses. Holy Spirit, I now ask that You would clearly show me any areas of personal weakness in which I must take action. Show me what I need to do to make progress in Your Kingdom.

(Now listen to what the Holy Spirit says and pay attention to the things He brings to mind. If someone who has hurt you in some way comes to your mind, forgive them and speak blessings over

them. After the Holy Spirit has revealed any areas of personal sin, you can continue this prayer.)

Father, please forgive me for (name the sin). I don't want to continue in passivity regarding this sin any longer. I don't want to carry around offenses and unforgiveness any longer. I release (name of person) from every offense. Bless (him/her), in Jesus' name. Grant me the grace to continue releasing others and to begin moving in obedience, leaving behind all things that would hinder my growth.

In the name of Jesus, I command any hindering spirits that have caused me to fail in times past to leave me now! I send you to the feet of Jesus! You will not bother me anymore! Go now!

Holy Spirit, come and fill me again with a fresh passion and courage to leave behind those things that hinder me and move ahead with renewed desire for the things of God. Thank You Lord for hearing my prayers and helping me in my weakness.

I ask all this in Jesus' name. Amen.

THE LORD'S WORD TO YOU

Dear awakening lion,

You have been gifted with the ability to begin discerning the differences between light and darkness in your own life. Let go of the darkness and I will lead you into greater light. I Myself am training you as the young lion you are, to take down lies with a vengeance. As you bind yourself to Me, you'll find both your authority and confidence increasing. Stay focused. Great victories lay ahead!

ENDNOTES

1. John Gill, *John Gill's Exposition of the Bible,* "Commentary on Revelation 21:19." http://biblestudy.crosswalk.com/ (accessed April 29, 2009.)

2. International Colored Gemstone Association. "Lapis Lazuli." http://www.gemstone.org/gem-by-gem/english/lapis.html (accessed April 29, 2009).

3. James Strong, *Strong's Exhaustive Concordance*. Hebrew: s.v. "cappiyr" 5601, 5608.

4. *The New Strong's Exhaustive Numbers and Concordance with Expanded Greek-Hebrew Dictionary*. CD-ROM. Biblesoft, Inc., and International Bible Translators, Inc., s.v. "forgive," (NT 630).

5. *The Zondervan Pictorial Bible Dictionary*, Zondervan Publishing House, 1967, Ur of the Chaldees, p. 876-877.

Chapter Four
Worshiping Warriors

TURQUOISE/CHALCEDONY—JUDAH'S STONE

The foundations of the wall of the city were adorned
with all kinds of precious stones:
the first foundation was jasper,
*the second sapphire, the third **chalcedony**...*
(Revelation 21:19).

It was getting late, so Terrie, a full-time employee for Boeing in the Seattle, Washington, area, decided it was time to go to bed. As she opened her bedroom door, she was shocked to see a large teardrop-shaped gemstone sitting neatly on top of her bed. The dark green stone had streaks of brown and black swirling across its faceted top. Nearly three inches long, the heavy stone appeared to be mountain jade, but she wasn't sure.

This was one of many stones Terrie and her husband had begun to find on a regular basis beginning in the fall of 2006. At first, she suspected her husband as the originator of the oddly placed gemstones; and he suspected her. But as the weeks turned into months, more and more gemstones kept appearing. Eventually, they had to acknowledge this as a work of God.

One of the more unique gemstones that appeared at their home is one a gemologist has deemed a geological impossibility. The heart-shaped stone features four completely different stones, amethyst, heliodor, pink sapphire, and emerald, with all four fused together as one.

When looking at the fourth gemstone, listed as *chalcedony* in some translations of the Bible, we find that a number of modern-day gemstones may also be included as a possibility for this stone (from Pliny the Elder's description in his A.D. 77 book, *Naturalis Historia*—Latin for "natural history"). Also, jade—like the stone found by Terrie—or even turquoise, could possibly be the stones used on the high priest's breastplate and those seen by John in the gemstone wall.

JUDAH, TRIBE OF PRAISE

Dance and celebration have always been an integral part of Israel's extensive history, so it comes as no surprise to see turquoise or chalcedony representing Judah's dance of praise. As we blossom into worshiping warriors of the Kingdom, we find walls of resistance beginning to crumble before us while shouts of praise erupt from within!

Historically, turquoise has been recognized as a gemstone from as early as 3000 B.C. Egyptian tombs have been discovered containing pieces of this "people's gemstone" inside.[1] Normally, sky-blue to grey-green in color with fine black spider-web veins running through it, the stone has been used to decorate everything from daggers and horse bridles to turbans. The name *turquoise* simply means "Turkish stone" and has been a popular token of friendship throughout the years.[2]

Ancient Egyptian artisans were sometimes known to take chalcedony or agate stones of poor quality and boil them in honey in order to deepen and intensify their coloring. Many centuries later, the Germans developed their artificial coloring techniques to such a degree that they were able to imitate more desirable gems such as chrysoprase or lapis lazuli.[3]

In biblical terms, the position of chalcedony or turquoise as the third foundation stone is very significant as it symbolizes the completeness of the triune Godhead, the Father, Son, and Holy Spirit. The Greek word for "chalcedony" in Revelation 21:19 is *chalkedon,* meaning "copper-like."[4] Therefore, indications are that this was possibly a yellowish variety of turquoise now found in China.

When examining the implications of this stone in our Christian growth, we find the Greek root further describes a "hollowing out" process.[5] Hollowing out indicates an emptying of self or a state of humility. The definition also mentions a chasm or impassable interval.[6]

Pride, the root of nearly all sin, is something that must be dealt with in order for the Holy Spirit to further permeate us (see 1 John 2:16). Without this necessary humbling process, we can progress no further. It is as though God has placed an impassable canyon of humility before us that must be walked through—a place of being laid low before God and others.

There are no shortcuts.

In our humiliation, a desperation for the Holy Spirit's assistance is established. Many times, when faced with our weaknesses and inabilities, we are forced to lift our hands in surrender to God's will and God's way in a particular circumstance. This type of surrender is precious in God's eyes, a true sacrifice of praise.

When studying the definitions of Judah, we discover its Hebrew translation indicates a celebration of worship where hands are used to both worship God and cast things out as necessary.[7] This again is a perfect description of a believer's life as he or she goes through God's sanctification process. We yield to God and worship Him with our hands. When the ways of the world or demonic forces try to oppress us, we lay our hands upon each other and cast them out. We see this enacted for us when Jesus instructs us in Matthew 10:8 to "heal the sick, cleanse the lepers, raise the dead, cast out demons. Freely you have received, freely give."

In Genesis 49:9, Jacob also describes Judah as a lion's whelp, but the cub is then seen crouching down preparing to attack his prey. When the battle is over, the cub's victory causes others to recognize the cub now as a mature lion. Moses declared in Deuteronomy 33:7 that God will hear the praises of Judah and will respond by sending help in battle. As God's authority is established in Judah, Judah is promised protection and aid in upcoming battles against his enemies.

First Thessalonians 5:23-24 further describes this portion of the sanctification process:

> *Now may the God of peace Himself sanctify you completely; and may your whole spirit, soul, and body be preserved blameless at the coming of our Lord Jesus Christ. He who calls you is faithful, who also will do it.*

As we learn to yield and cast out things that don't belong in our lives, we grow. More and more of our inner man is being transformed daily.

GOOD LEAVEN, BAD LEAVEN

Leaven is something Jesus used to help us understand sanctification in the Kingdom of God. One parable about the good leaven of truth and humility is found both in Luke 13:21 and Matthew 13:33. Jesus explains that the Kingdom of Heaven is like leaven. The woman in this story places leaven in three measures of meal (or flour) and then allows it to slowly transform the flour into edible bread. I believe the three measures of meal symbolize the three parts of a human being: body, soul, and spirit—the parts that are being sanctified.

Once the leaven of truth has been placed and left undisturbed within an individual, truth will begin to permeate every part of that person. In First Corinthians 5:8 the unleavened bread of sincerity and truth describes the type of *leavening* God is looking for. True humility and brokenness before God are represented by the ground-up meal. By allowing the Holy Spirit to fully penetrate us, we will eventually be filled with God's presence in every area of our lives.

In Matthew 16:6, Jesus warns His disciples about another kind of leaven, a deadly form that may initially appear to be the same as the good leaven. He called this *"the leaven of the Pharisees and the Sadducees."* Luke 12:1 indicates that this leaven of the Pharisees is actually hypocrisy; while First Corinthians 5:8 further describes it as *"the leaven of malice and wickedness."*

The hypocrisy of the Pharisees and Sadducees was demonstrated by their behavior as they went to great lengths to impress each other with their outward religious appearances. Sadly, their hearts were not yielded to God and Jesus knew it. Later, He referred to them as *"whitewashed tombs... full of dead men's bones... "* (Matt. 23:27). They were clean on the outside while dead on the inside.

From this contrast of the two leavens, we come to understand that merely following the law of religious behavior does not indicate a true transformation in the inward parts. God is not impressed with our outward demonstrations of "godly devotion." He is concerned with our hearts. His goal is to grow us up in sincerity and humility. This is the foundation of truth that He must have in order for us to move on into Kingdom maturity.

Just as the Israelites were forced to wander around in the wilderness until the roots of doubt, unbelief, and fear died out in their generation, the Lord will delay our next stage of development until we have learned the current lesson. We too can be wandering around the mountain until we embrace the impassable canyon of humility. Our Father is very creative in coming up with ways and methods of humbling us so we can move ahead with the right attitude before Him. He wants us to depend upon Him for everything, and at the same time, He desires us to learn how to use His authority properly.

BALANCE HUMILITY AND AUTHORITY

In the midst of an attack when our children were very young, I had to learn to strike the balance between necessary humility and the proper use of authority.

With no warning, I found myself suddenly afflicted with severe lower-back pain. The pain was so intense that I fell to the floor unable to move my legs without screaming in pain. Our young boys watched as I dragged myself over to the phone to call for help.

Shortly afterward, both my mother and husband came rushing into the house to check on me. With their help, I walked out to our van and was rushed to the emergency room. After the examination, the doctor first looked at John standing nervously at my side.

"Do you work?" he asked my husband. We were both a little taken back by this question.

"Yes," John replied. He had just started a new job in building and grounds maintenance with our church.

"Well, not any more," the doctor responded. "Your wife can do absolutely nothing for six weeks. You need to stay home and take care of her."

We were in shock! The doctor explained I had torn the ligaments in my lower back and they needed time to heal. I was instructed to stay in bed while taking pain pills and muscle relaxants to help ease the discomfort. A heating pad had to be placed on my back day and night.

However, the bad news did not stop there.

The doctor believed that, even after six weeks of bed rest, I would continue to suffer chronic back pain, most likely for the rest of my life. I would not be able to lift more than ten pounds, even after I recovered. Most devastating to me was the news that I would not be able to pick up or hold either of our two boys, as this would injure my back further. Darkness hung over both of us like a heavy blanket as we wondered how this might affect all our plans for the future.

We were desperate!

The week after my injury passed at a snail's pace. John attempted to keep me immobile in obedience to the doctor's orders for bed rest. Completely dependent on my husband for everything, I was in a position for God to humble me in many ways.

In spite of all the bad news, somehow I still had a glimmer of hope for a miracle. I knew I had a family that needed me, so after receiving prayer from one of the pastors at our church, I started pushing myself to get up and begin moving again.

Within a week or so, I could walk around stiffly and with minimal pain. Soon, I had recovered sufficiently so that my husband could return to work. Throughout the months and years that followed, I learned to be careful while lifting heavy objects to avoid a relapse of back pain. Functionally, my life was pretty much back to normal. We even had two more children; but the battle was not completely over.

Though I was active and basically healthy, every couple of months or so a paralyzing pain would grip my lower back causing me to be bedridden (actually couch-ridden) for several days at a time. Eventually, the pain would subside and I would be back to normal. For many years, I assumed this was as far as God's healing would take me. However, the Lord had a much bigger plan, as well as a huge lesson for me to learn through all this.

One Sunday morning, we were all at church enjoying an energetic worship service when spontaneous dancing broke out in the congregation. It was so wonderful to see the freedom of God being expressed by both the young and old in our church. I wanted to join in. Almost immediately, I heard a voice as clear as anything.

"If you dance, you'll hurt your back," it threatened me.

Somehow I knew who was speaking to me and it was not the Lord. A godly anger rose up inside. All I knew was that I needed to respond in exactly the opposite manner to what that voice was telling me. I was sick of this four-year assault against me!

Under my breath, I reminded the devil that I had given my life and my entire body to the Lord. My back belonged to the Lord and the enemy had no authority over the Lord's back. Once that truth was declared, I moved in agreement with my Healer and joined the others in dancing freely before God. That was the end of my lower-back attacks.

As I reflect on this experience, I see the Lord's grace in first humbling me *before* I could finally learn how to use His authority in defeating the enemy. It obviously took some time for the leaven of humility to work its way through my pile of meal. (There was definitely more to come!) Once I had been humbled and broken of my self-sufficiency, God's authority rose up within me and I was granted the victory. Praise God!

Turquoise, with its swirls of green, yellow, and black markings reminds me of my sacrifice of praise and worship rising up like trails of incense before the Lord. The more I yield and surrender to His ways in my life, the more sanctified I become, which in turn brings greater joy to my Father.

The green colors of turquoise can represent life coming through the counsel of God, while yellow demonstrates the understanding He grants us like the early morning rays breaking through the darkness.[8] Sanctification as represented by turquoise truly is a beautiful thing!

Learning to function as a true worshiper of God and gaining spiritual battle skills against the onslaught of our enemy are truly lifelong processes. The enemy's purpose in every attack is to get our eyes off Jesus and change our focus from faith to fear. However, God has a purpose in allowing us to face our battles: It is to gain confidence in Him so that we are able to worship the King with abandon...even in the midst of an attack.

REFLECTIONS ON THE ROCK

We are told that *"perfect love casts out fear"* (1 John 4:18). Therefore, as we develop our complete love and trust in the Lord, every fiber of our being is slowly being transformed into His image. Humility is the key. Pride leads only to death.

Our greatest victories are always achieved in true humility. Humility acknowledges that every gift comes from the hand of God and all gifts are available as He deems them necessary. If we are engaged in a God-directed spiritual battle, we can be confident that the Spirit of God will rise up on our behalf granting us His authority to overcome.

"Faith muscles" are developed through each encounter—whether we gain the manifestation of victory or experience failure (usually because we have moved in our own understanding!). Both outcomes serve as valuable learning tools for the future. As our authority increases, we will be asked to move into larger arenas of spiritual battle.

Many of us feel as though we are completely inadequate to become true worshipers of the King or engage in spiritual battle. The enemy loves to fill our minds with all kinds of lies about our unworthiness or inability to move into this turquoise stage of development. Since we now understand that only the blood of Jesus makes us worthy and only the gifts of God enable us to do all things, let's face down the enemy's lies and replace them with the truth.

LET'S PRAY!

Lord Jesus, I come before You and humbly ask for Your forgiveness. I have chosen to believe lies from the enemy about myself and my abilities. I repent of these deceptions and ask You to wash me clean in Your blood.

In the name of Jesus, I come against the sense of unworthiness and all insecurities that cause me to walk in fear and doubt. Devil, you are a liar! I command you to leave me and go to the feet of Jesus now! I don't want you anymore! I now choose to believe only what God says about me.

Holy Spirit, I now ask that You fill me with a desire to become a true worshiper of my Father. Grant me the grace to take on any spiritual challenges put in my path. I know You will give me all that I need to gain the ultimate victory.

Thank You, Lord for all You do and for who You are. In Jesus' name I pray. Amen

THE LORD'S WORD TO YOU

Dear worshiping warrior,

I have watched as you exercised my gift of authority to conquer the enemy of your soul in many areas. It brings Me great joy to see you grow in skill and wisdom. Remember that your greatest strength comes in worshiping Me. When your soul is filled with My presence, you will open your hands and see My power flow through you. Though engaged in warfare, you will find peace in knowing that I am your source, your authority, your power. Let Me work through you as your willingness to yield to My will increases.

ENDNOTES

1. Texas Natural Science Center: Non-vertebrate Paleontology Laboratory, "Rocks and Minerals." http://www.utexas.edu/tmm/npl/mineralogy/lore_and_myt hology/index.html (accessed April 29, 2009).

2. International Colored Gemstones Association: Gem by Gem, "Turquoise." www.gemstone.org/gem/english/turquoise.htm (accessed April 29, 2009); Rings and Things, www.rings-things.com/gemstone/t.htm (accessed April 29, 2009).

3. Ruth V. Wright and Robert L. Chadbourne, *Crystals, Gems & Minerals of the Bible* (New Canaan, CT: Keats Publishing, Inc., 1970), 32.

4. *The New Strong's Exhaustive Numbers and Concordance with Expanded Greek-Hebrew Dictionary.* CD-ROM. Biblesoft, Inc., and International Bible Translators, Inc., s.v. "chalkedon," (NT 5472).

5. Ibid., s.v. "chalkos" (NT 5475).

6. James Strong, *Strong's Exhaustive Concordance,* Greek #5465, *chalao,* #5490, *chasma.*

7. *The New Strong's Exhaustive Numbers and Concordance with Expanded Greek-Hebrew Dictionary.* CD-ROM. Biblesoft, Inc., and International Bible Translators, Inc., s.v. "Y'huwdaah" (OT 3063) and s.v. "yadah" (OT 3034).

8. Some dear friends had some amazing experiences where the Lord revealed the meaning of each color in the rainbow. They are currently working on their own book describing this and other experiences. They've even had the glory cloud of the Lord descend upon their home and sit in their living room for over a week! People entering their home were not able to stand as God's presence was so strong.

Chapter Five

Living Stones

EMERALD/GARNET—LEVI'S STONE

And He who sat there was like
a jasper and sardius stone in appearance;
and there was a rainbow around the throne,
*in appearance like an **emerald** (Revelation 4:3).*

Several years ago, things began changing for Pastor Len and his congregation. It all started with eight weeks of special meetings held at his church. That's when feathers began randomly falling during their services amidst healings, miracles, and a number of salvations. And then there was the gold dust. Who could explain that? However, the thing that seemed to top it all began in late 2007 when perfect little gemstones began falling throughout the church sanctuary.[1]

"We could hear the gemstones hitting the chairs and then bouncing to the floor," Pastor Len explained.

Some of the gemstones were diamonds and some were amethyst stones; all were about half the size of a fingernail. One of the amethyst stones was taken to a jeweler who confirmed its authenticity and estimated its value at around $30.

Earlier that morning as they were praying for an associate pastor's wife, several witnesses saw small diamonds forming in the air above her head and dropping into her hair. It took them quite a while to pick out each of the sparkling diamonds from her hair.[2]

Most recently, Pastor Len was heavy in prayer for a sick member of his congregation. The weight of that burden wore him down as he continued in intercession for some time. As the time drew near for him to head to the church that night, he asked the Lord for a sign of encouragement.

Heading toward the bedroom where his jacket was lying on the bed, something caught his eye. Sitting on the bed next to his jacket was a beautifully faceted amethyst gemstone similar to the ones they had been finding at the church. Instantly, he knew this was the sign he had asked for; he left for the church greatly encouraged!

THE EMERALD IN HISTORY

We can also find great encouragement as we examine the fourth layer of foundation stones in the wall surrounding New Jerusalem. According to Revelation 21:19, that stone is *emerald*.

At least one expert believes that the emerald referred to in the Bible may have actually been a green garnet as it was more readily available in Bible times.[3] According to the Jewish Encyclopedia, this emerald may have been assigned to the tribe of Levi.

By examining the definition of *Levi*—found in the *Strong's Exhaustive Concordance* (attached to *twine, unite, remain, borrow, to lend, cleave*)—and by noting the similarities of meaning for this fourth level in the book *Interpreting the Symbols and Types* by Kevin Conner, I believe the emerald may have been assigned to this tribe. Even Jewish scholars admit that the exact identification, order of the stones, and tribes they were assigned to is a matter of speculation.

In Deuteronomy 33:8-10, we discover promises given by Moses addressing the people of this tribe. Moses acknowledged Levi as being in a desert place or time of testing. Yet, he also states that God's truth would be entrusted to Levi throughout this period. As a result of overcoming difficulties while learning to become a "living sacrifice," the tribe of Levi would become teachers of God's Word to others.

Ancient cultures throughout history have used the emerald as a symbol of spring and tranquility. Both Cleopatra and Julius Caesar fancied the stone, but for different reasons. Cleopatra often wore the gems as enhancements to her legendary beauty while Julius Caesar wore them believing that the stones had curative powers.[5]

Garnets are found in shades of red, blue, and green. These varieties have been widely regarded and used as gemstones for thousands of years. They develop their various shades according to the kind of lighting to which they are exposed (including varying degrees of natural or artificial lighting now used in modern times).

In past ages, the garnet has been designated as a symbol of fire, faith, courage, truth, grace, compassion, constancy, and fidelity. Consequently, the garnet was best known as the warrior's stone.[6]

Legend has it that even Noah was attracted to the beauty of this stone. He supposedly suspended a finely cut glowing garnet in the ark to help bring light into their living quarters.[7] This legend likely came about as a result of the garnet's high rate of light refraction; this quality causes the stone to appear as though it were actually glowing. This "glowing" of the stone might serve as a reminder that we carry God's truth and glory in spite of the challenges we face.

From a biblical perspective, the garnet's placement in the fourth position represents the number of the earth. We are reminded that all life on this earth and even the earth itself proceeded from the Creator. Yet, all life remains dependent upon the grace and mercy of our God. Without Him, we would all cease to exist! (See Colossians 1:16-17.)

LEVI—THE SET-APART TRIBE

As we look further into the uniqueness of the tribe of Levi, we see a pattern of interdependence clearly portrayed. The Levites were set apart from the other tribes; this allowed them to concentrate on their service to God in the temple. This priestly service resulted in a special awareness of the presence of God as they fulfilled their duties each day. Working together as a team, the Levites were forced to rely upon one another and upon the other tribes in order to accomplish their tasks. Even their necessary sustenance was provided from a portion of the food offerings brought in by the other tribes.

The Body of Christ still functions through relationship. Peter uses the imagery of stones to describe us. We are told in First Peter 2:4-5 that we are *"living stones"* whom the Lord uses to build a spiritual house and establish His holy priesthood. This is a picture of interdependence, which the Bible calls an acceptable spiritual sacrifice.

It only stands to reason that one stone doesn't make a house. Several stones placed together in a heap also fail to qualify as a house. To build a house, one must have many stones laid one on top of another in proper order. Submission and dependence—each of the stones cooperating with and relying upon the others to maintain the integrity of the structure—are necessary for the house to be complete and livable.

By submitting one to another, we hold each other accountable for all that is going on in our lives. When one is weak, another is strong and able to encourage the vulnerable brother or sister. To keep our faith fresh and filled with renewed commitment, we need each other.

This interdependence also allows the unique talents or giftedness of individuals to flow freely within the structure of the spiritual house. With love, humility, and a teachable spirit serving as the mortar between the stones, this wall of living stones is able to stand strong, even against the blast of storm winds all of us face at one point or another.

Strength Against the Storms

Storms (trials) in the life of a believer are not something we would naturally look forward to; yet storms are another part of God's plan. Unnecessary things—the chaff and weak links in our lives—are revealed and even blown away in the midst of storms.

This is both a destructive and a building process. Bad things can be swept away and good things can be *blown in.* On some occasions, storms can also be designed as a witness to those around us as they see the deliverance of God in our lives. The role of storms often depends upon which spiritual season of life we may be in.

Matthew 24:31 speaks of four winds coming from the four corners of the earth; each can accomplish varying purposes as they blow through our lives.

The East Wind. Traditionally, the *east wind* symbolizes storms and the uncontrollable power of God. The east wind was known to wreck ships and destroy growing crops—not something we would necessarily desire. However, without a storm to calm, many of us might not fully understand the extent of God's authority over all venues of life.

The east wind might also be connected with the winter season when it appears as though everything has died and difficulties surround us on all sides. When the east wind hits, it's time to do as many of God's creatures do...find a place of rest and solace in the goodness of God to shelter us from the storms blowing all around us. God's purposes for us can be revealed even in the darkest of situations. It's up to us to find that secret place of peace and stay there until the darkness lifts.

Discovering God's plan in each challenging situation is crucial. Is His voice calling us to step out of our fears to join Him in walking on top of the stormy waters? Are we to speak to the storm to calm it? Can we be at peace even while treading water as Paul did when he was shipwrecked?

The Bible consoles us with the promise in Psalms 34:19 that *"many are the afflictions of the righteous, but the Lord delivers him out of them all."* In His time, we will be delivered. Meanwhile, we must seek His instructions and embrace whatever He desires to teach us throughout the trial.

In our own lives, my husband and I have suffered many seasons of affliction. Yet, looking back, we can see the hand of God through it all. We went through such a season of affliction, beginning with a traffic accident involving John's truck. On his way to a job site, he was rear-ended by an intoxicated driver; it was a hit-and-run collision. John's truck was totaled. Miraculously, he was uninjured and the driver was detained shortly afterward and identified in a second accident further down the highway.

The days that followed caused us to seek the Lord like never before. We had been praying that the Lord would reveal to us His plan for our lives at this time by shutting the doors He did not desire for us. Consequently, each time my husband attempted to buy a replacement work truck, the truck was sold before he got there. This happened five times in a row! Without a truck, he wasn't able to continue his work in construction.

God had our attention! He made it very clear to both of us that this was our season of change. Through the challenging circumstances that followed, we began experiencing a fresh stirring in our spirits and increased desire for His presence. The direction of our lives was altered as a result of this trial.

The North Wind. In Bible times, the north wind brought rain and was considered a season of refreshment as this wind was free of humidity.[8] Typically, winter is followed by spring so it makes sense that the Lord would follow an east wind season with times of refreshing. The Lord never allows us to go through more than we can handle in any given trial, though we may *think* it's too much at the time. His ultimate purpose in all of our lives is to see us grow up into His character. Each of our trials is uniquely designed to help us move on with Him. Then He refreshes our weary spirits for a season before moving us on to the next challenge.

The South Wind. When the Lord sees changes in our hearts, He mercifully sends a south wind to blow gently and encourage this new growth. These soothing and purifying breezes bring a breath of fresh air to the work of God going on in our hearts. The south wind might be compared to summer when gentle breezes blow just enough to cool the sweating brow. In this "summer" season, the sun shines and we advance rapidly in the Kingdom of God.

The West Wind. As we know from past experiences, we have an enemy who is continually attempting to rob us of the good seed of truth being sown in our hearts by the Holy Spirit. The devil can do this with a contrary wind or simply by choking out spiritual growth with the cares or worries of this life. When the doors of sin are opened in our lives, the enemy tries to overwhelm us with "plagues" that attack us through doubt or unbelief. This is when the Lord releases His west winds; these are winds that blow away the assaults against our souls—similar to what happens in the fall season where the wind blows off the dead and dying leaves from the trees to prepare them for the days ahead.

The feeding of the 4,000 in the wilderness and the resurrection of Lazarus after four days in the tomb remind us during this season of "fours" that our God specializes in "impossible" situations and uses them to further teach us of His power. We would never have the opportunity to see and experience this side of our loving Father if there were not a wilderness experience or even a season of fears and darkness preceding the revelation of God's glory in our lives.

While we cannot fully understand the purposes of God in every situation, we can be assured that our Father always has our well-being in mind as He walks us through the *"valley of the shadow of death"* (Ps. 23:4). Though we cannot see, we choose to believe. This is the essence of our faith. Without this kind of faith, we can never please God (see Heb. 11:6).

Both the vibrant green emerald and the multi-hued garnet stones can remind us of the promised life that only springs forth after the seed has died in the ground. For those who have experienced the forgiveness of sin through Jesus Christ, the dark red of the most popular garnet variety can remind us of the shed blood of our Savior as He paid for both our healing and our redemption.

As warriors in the Kingdom of God, we too, can carry the emerald or garnet as a symbol of the authority granted us as joint heirs with Jesus, even as we face whatever storms come our way. We bravely move ahead in spiritual conquests while locking arms with our brothers and sisters in Christ. We truly are to be dependent and interdependent in this family of living stones.

Matthew 24:31 says: *"And He will send His angels with a great sound of a trumpet, and they will gather together His elect from the four winds, from one end of heaven to the other."* As we learned in this chapter, the four winds represent four different spiritual seasons in which believers may find themselves. These seasons vary depending upon what the Lord deems necessary to keep us dependent on Him and interdependent within the Body of Christ.

REFLECTIONS ON THE ROCK

Many of us are tempted to become spiritual "lone rangers" who never allow others within the Body of Christ to share their spiritual giftings with us. It's easy to fall into the lie of believing we are somehow above everyone else and need only to hear from God directly. That is a dangerous place to be. That is a form of pride; a multitude of other deceptions can easily slip in behind it. Before we know it, the enemy can lead us down a trail of unnecessary pain and self-destruction.

True humility and repentance are tools created by our Father to provide a way of escape from the snares of the enemy. By humbling ourselves before God and humanity, the Lord will ultimately exalt us to the position of service for which He created us, safely situated within His wall of living stones.

LET'S PRAY!

Dear Jesus, I first want to humble myself before You and ask for Your forgiveness for having allowed pride and many other things to separate me from Your Body. I ask You to wash me in Your blood that I might be cleansed from all the lies that have caused me to walk in independence rather than interdependence. I choose the way of humility before You and Your Body.

Holy Spirit, I now ask You to search my heart and show me any other areas of pride in which I need to repent. (If "pictures" of people or incidents come to mind at this time pause and consider them; they are most likely indications that you need to forgive, or ask forgiveness from, specific people.)

Lord, I ask You to forgive me for my offenses against (insert names). Grant me the gift of forgiveness for those who have offended me so that I might walk in true humility before them as You desire. I know You want me to love as You love. Please grant me Your gift of love for those You have placed in my life, especially those within Your Body. Teach me how to find my position within Your Body so we all might function the way You have planned from the very beginning.

Thank You for all of these things, in Jesus' name. Amen.

The Lord's Word to You

Dear child of My refining,

Though it seems as though you go through challenge after challenge, know that I will never test you beyond your ability to endure. I understand that, at times, it may feel as though you cannot withstand your circumstances any longer; but remember: I am both smoking out the works of the flesh and establishing you within My Body. You need Me and you need others in My Body to encourage and build you up during this time. This is My way.

This season of testing will not endure forever. The offering of your life to Me is a sweet fragrance before Me. Know that when you emerge from this desert, My truth and glory will shine through you like never before. You will be fashioned into a straight arrow that can easily be shot wherever it's needed. Remember, My eyes are always upon you. My wall of protection is continually about you.

ENDNOTES

1. Telephone interview, April 2008. This was confirmed by two other individuals who were also there.

2. Telephone interview, April 2008. Confirmed by two other individuals also present that day.

3. James Strong, *Strong's Exhaustive Concordance,* "Emerald" Hebrew #5306.

4. Ruth V. Wright and Robert L. Chadbourne, *Crystals, Gems & Minerals of the Bible* (New Canaan, CT: Keats Publishing, Inc., 1970), 57-58.

5. Morris Jastrow Jr., Ira Maurice Price, Marcus Jastrow Louis Ginzberg, *Jewish Encyclopedia,* http://www.jewishencyclopedia .com/view.jsp?artid=1433&letter=B&search=breastplate %20stones

6. Rings & Things, http://www.rings-things.com/gemstone/ g.htm (accessed April, 29, 2009).

7. Ibid.

8. These winds are based on the winds blowing in Israel. *The Zondervan Pictorial Bible Dictionary* (Colorado Springs, CO: Zondervan Publishing, 1967), 894.

Chapter Six

The Overcomer Prevails

Onyx/Sardonyx—Joseph's Stone

*Then you shall take two **onyx** stones*
and engrave on them the names
of the sons of Israel... (Exodus 28:9).

Carla, a traveling minister, had heard much about the beautiful gemstones appearing in churches and homes globally, so when a friend mentioned the idea of visiting a local couple who had received many gemstones, she was thrilled! The day finally came for their visit and Carla was overwhelmed with what she saw.

The variety of gemstones, both large and small, surprised her. She learned that three more gemstones had been found near the couple's front door just the evening before. During their visit, the couple, in obedience to the voice of the Lord, gave Carla one of the new arrivals, a large purple stone, to share with other churches to which she would minister in the future.

The stone itself was about the size of a small walnut and fit quite comfortably in the palm of her hand. The weightiness of the stone surprised her as it was heavier than one might expect from a stone of that size.

(Some attribute the additional weight of the heavenly gemstones to the "weight" of God's glory resting upon them.)

The cuts and facets of this stone, however, seemed very unusual. She began showing her gemstone in churches all over the United States. Carla soon saw that the more she showed the unique gemstone, the more the stone itself seemed to sparkle and grow in beauty, right before her eyes! She was amazed at how many ways the stone seemed to capture the light and flash with color, thrilling all who saw it.[1]

As we consider this story, we can see how easy it is for many of us to take the gifts God gives and unwittingly undervalue them with questions such as, *Why didn't God give me a flashier gift?* or *Why couldn't I be called to do something else like so-and-so was?*

The truth, however, is that, if we will begin to use what He has given us, the true beauty of the gift will be revealed; the appreciation of others and the beauty of our own growth in spiritual maturity will cause our gifts to sparkle and shine like never before!

THE VALUE OF SMALL BEGINNINGS

Both Carla's gemstone and the early years of Joseph's adult life may have appeared unappealing at first. However, with God we discover the true beauty of what He is doing only as the story progresses and the wisdom of His preparation for our future days is revealed.

In Joseph's case, his willingness to trust God despite difficult circumstances resulted in his ability to save both his family and the nation of Egypt from starvation during the drought. How amazing is that!

Overcoming great obstacles has always been a characteristic of the heroes of our faith. Things almost never are as they first appear to us in the natural. In Joseph's case, what appeared to be a miserable life of separation from his family and hopeless subjection to the harshness of slavery, proved to be something quite different later on.

Recalling Joseph's story of undying faith can both bless and inspire us as we examine the stones of onyx or sardonyx (the distinction will be explained below), the stones most likely assigned to the tribe of Joseph, (the eleventh son assigned the eleventh stone on the breastplate) and the fifth stone in the wall's foundation.[2]

Many great promises were given to the tribe of Joseph by Jacob in Genesis 49:22-26. These verses detail the deep grieving over which Joseph prevailed—and the strength that flowed through him as God removed all pride and arrogance from his heart. Great fruitfulness and eternal blessings were proclaimed over the generations that followed. This was the result of Joseph's humble submission and unquestioning faith in God.

Deuteronomy 33:13-17 details the favor of God even while Joseph was in the midst of dark circumstances. In these verses Moses spoke of the blessings of the east.[3] By looking at the previous chapter we understand this blessing refers to the hidden treasures of God that are only discovered during apparently destructive events we face in life.

Joseph's willingness to accept the plan of God resulted in two specific promises. The first was the reaping of "double blessings" (the definition of Ephraim's name). The second promise was that these blessings would literally cause him to forget the anguish of his past trials (the definition of Manassah's name).[4]

Onyx, From the Beginning

As the first stone mentioned in the Bible, we find onyx listed along with gold in Genesis 2:12. This stone was selected by the Lord to have all 12 names of the tribes engraved into it. Ancient Greeks and Romans used onyx for both cameos and intaglios[5] (carvings made into the stone opposite of cameos), as the contrasting white layers on top and darker layers underneath made a perfect backdrop for lapidary works of art. Some Middle Easterners considered onyx to be "a worry stone," believing it supposedly absorbed negative energy. We understand the only biblical solution to worry involves casting all our cares upon the Lord Himself and allowing Him to take care of us as He has promised (see 1 Pet. 5:7).

Early Roman writers also referred to sardonyx as a "gem of great value." It was a common practice among lawyers of that day to rent costly sardonyx rings in order to appear prosperous and convey an extravagant lifestyle. Reportedly, even Julius Caesar was an enthusiastic collector of the beautifully engraved stones.[6]

Onyx itself is a semiprecious variety of agate with white, black, brown, or red alternating bands of color throughout the stone. The name *onyx* originates from a Greek word meaning "fingernail"[7] or "hoof." The use of the word *sardonyx*[8] in the Book of Revelation indicates that onyx with red bands (*sard*) was the variety referred to.

This stone carries an important message to the Church as we take notice of the precise layering of contrasting colors. Black onyx, I believe, can represent the works of humankind on this earth while the stratum of red (or white) symbolizes the grace of God repeatedly covering humanity with His favor. The weakness of humankind then becomes God's strength in us. This symbolism is confirmed as the number five also points to the cross and God's grace to humankind.

When looking into the life of Joseph, we see what appear to be multiple devastations heaped upon an innocent victim of jealousy (see Gen. 37; 39–47). One might think that his only fault was accepting the position of favored son among 11 brothers. However, there were many things God was specifically targeting in order to prepare this young man for the extraordinary position of power that lay ahead of him.

Harsh circumstances are many times necessary in order to develop strength and godly character within an individual. Such was the case with Joseph.

Though he suffered much, the end of his story speaks volumes as we see how God lavished many blessings upon him in his season of reaping. So it can be with us—if we are willing to accept God's plan and God's way within our lives.

FIVE WISE VIRGINS, FIVE UNWISE

In continuing our study into the significance of the number *five,* we find two groups of five in the parable of the ten virgins described in Matthew 25:1-13. All ten virgins were awaiting the arrival of the bridegroom. Though all the virgins started out with lamps full of oil, only five of them were wise enough to keep their lamps trimmed by bringing an extra supply of oil with them. The five foolish virgins were not prepared for the delay they encountered; they consequently missed the arrival of the bridegroom and were left—shut out in darkness.

The five wise and five foolish virgins serve as reminders to carefully guard our passion for the things of God throughout any delays in the Lord's return. His grace is available, but we need to remain single-minded about the Lord and His purposes for us on this earth. If we don't embrace His lessons and instruction, the enemy will rob us and the "stolen" fruit will not mature in our lives (see Matt. 13:4,19). The failure to allow His truths to penetrate every area of our hearts can become the source of our demise in future times of testing (see Matt. 13:5-7;19-22).

The parable of the virgins ends with the words *"watch therefore"* (Matt. 25:13), so we naturally have to ask, "What are we to watch for?"

The word *watch* in Matthew 25:13 refers to keeping oneself awake or rousing oneself from sleep or from sitting or lying in disease or death.[9] It's clear that inactivity in spiritual affairs leads to spiritual dullness.

A verse found in Second Corinthians 13:5 gives us further insight as Paul exhorted the Corinthians to examine themselves daily to make certain they were still walking in faith. If not resisted, the corruption of this world which surrounds us will affect both our spiritual and physical bodies.

In the case of the wise virgins, successful tending of their lamps might have been the result of responding to the encouragement and promptings of their companions.

"Look," I can imagine one saying to the other, "your flame is growing dim. Do you need to add oil or adjust the wick?"

The five wise virgins were very focused on their lamps so the allotted oil would last until the call came. On the other hand, it's obvious that the condition of the lamps and the burning wicks were not a huge priority to the five foolish virgins. As the hour grew late, they must have allowed their love of comfort to lull them to sleep; and while they rested, their oil ran out.

Unfortunately, instead of making the genuine pursuit of the Lord and His will for our lives top priority, many of us base our life decisions on personal comfort. If we surround ourselves with "comfortable" believers, is it possible that all of us would grow lazy together and neglect the great gift of God's grace? This question is a sobering one for us to consider.

Had the five foolish virgins heeded the warnings of the five wise ones, I'm sure they would have done something to ensure they had enough oil for themselves. Instead, it seemed easier to try and take from the five wise virgins the oil they lacked. The unwise virgins, however, failed to realize that it was too late to take the easy way out; the wise virgins only had enough oil for themselves.

When their laxness was not rewarded, the foolish virgins quickly went searching for more oil. It ended up costing them their admittance into the wedding feast. I can imagine their heartsick panic at the gate when the bridegroom said, *"Assuredly, I say to you, I do not know you"* (Matt. 25:12).

FIVE TALENTS

Another significant example of *five* found in the New Testament has to do with the five talents given to the first of three servants called to do their master's bidding in Matthew 25:14-30.

A second servant is given three talents and the third, just one talent. The point of the parable seems to be that the three servants were asked to step out and use what the master had given them to advance his kingdom. Two of the servants were faithful; they used their talents wisely to the king's benefit. However, the third servant allowed fear to paralyze him. He did nothing with what he was given. When the master returned, the third servant was stripped of the single talent and punished.

The story of the servants in this parable and in a similar story found in Luke 19:11-27 indicates that the Lord expects us to make progress and grow spiritually in the Kingdom of God while we're here on earth. He is not pleased with someone who's content and comfortable doing only what they've done in years past. To properly apply the grace and mercy of God upon our lives is to infer that we must experience growth and increase as we exercise each new truth He reveals to us. His grace gives us new freedom, allowing us to conquer new territories personally and to have a greater impact on others eternally.

All of us have received from God "talents" in one form or another; He *expects* us to use them, even when it means leaving our comfort zones. There was just such a time in my life when I could feel the uncomfortable push of the Holy Spirit prompting me to move into a new area of influence over others...and I *really* was not eager to move.

After 13 years of home schooling my own children, I was asked to step in as a substitute teacher for a sixth-grade class in a local Christian school. They were desperate and needed someone to fill in for the remaining three weeks of school as the former teacher had suddenly resigned. I didn't know what I had gotten myself into when I agreed to help out, but the Holy Spirit was already at work and it was time for me to move up into a new level of ministry.

Feeling woefully inadequate for the task, I walked into the classroom of 20 students, all of whom were either 12 or 13 years old. It was evident that they were looking to test me as they had every prior teacher for the previous several years. The question was, Would they break me, too? I quickly learned that this class had a reputation as "the worst class in the school." Their behavior that first day quickly affirmed that this might be true.

The battle had begun. What these students didn't know about me was that I was a spiritual warrior for the souls of those around me. My motto while raising our own children had always been that when it came to a battle of wills, they would never win. The Holy Spirit was able to take that same tenacity and direct it toward this group of unruly and rebellious hearts.

After the first day of assessing the situation, my husband and I sat down to discuss the challenges I was facing. He suggested I use the law to reestablish God's standards in the classroom. Immediately, I sat down and devised a lesson plan that presented each of the Ten Commandments at the beginning of our school day before moving on to other subjects.

Each day, I hammered those hardened hearts with a New Testament interpretation of God's law and each day I ended the lesson stating that this demonstrated why we needed Jesus so desperately. No one was able to fully live a sin-free life without the blood of Jesus and the grace He provided for us to conduct ourselves in godly ways. I challenged each of them to talk with me during recess if they desired to make things right with the Lord.

After ten days of the law, their walls of resistance finally began to crumble. One morning, a couple of the boys met me at recess to ask if they could pray with me in the chapel. Of course, I was greatly encouraged by this and took the boys in for prayer; but I was not prepared for what happened next.

Once we entered the chapel, both boys began to cry and travail before God as the conviction of the Holy Spirit moved upon them. Realizing this would not end quickly, I grabbed my husband (the school's pastor) and another associate pastor and asked them to stay with the boys while I collected the other children from the schoolyard.

When the other children heard that two of the boys were praying in the chapel, they insisted on joining them. Unconvinced of their sincerity and believing they were trying to avoid schoolwork, I at first refused the request. Yet, they continued asking, so I decided to take all of them in for a time of prayer. Prior to entering the chapel, I warned my students that if I saw anyone not praying during this time, we would leave and return to the classroom.

Hearing the travail of the two boys in the front, the students soberly entered the church. I watched as they broke up into small groups, positioning themselves around the chapel. Within moments, we could see the Spirit of God move over these young hearts. Soft cries of repentance first began in one group and then moved to the next one. Before long, nearly everyone was crying as God was doing a tender work in their hearts.

The days that followed were absolutely amazing. The class that was once considered impossible to work with was being transformed before our eyes. They were humble and broken before God. Their behavior changed dramatically. The only battle I now had was trying to balance their constant desire to pray in the chapel with finishing out their school curriculum for the year.

What an incredible thing to witness! God's mercy was poured out and many lives were changed, even while I was challenged to believe God for the ability to meet this spiritual battle head-on. All of us grew as a result of God's unmerited favor lavished upon us.

BENEFITS IN THE "GOOD LAND"

The onyx can remind us that God's mercy and favor are but a prayer away. His gifts and talents have already been placed within each of us; but it is how we use what God has given that will determine His response to us in the future.

As we wear Joseph's stone, we can meditate on the unwavering faith he maintained even through his many ordeals. The trials he faced helped prepare him for his future position of favor; and in the end Joseph received the blessings promised him in Deuteronomy 33:13-17. So can we!

As you consider the significance of onyx, remember also, that the stone appears early in the first book of the Bible. Genesis 2:11-12 said onyx was found in the *"good land"* of Havilah, a circle representing the earth. Gold and bdellium (an aromatic resin) were also found there.

Gold represents the glory of God and man's purification process. Bdellium represents the fragrance of God and the prayers of the saints continually coming up before the throne of God. Onyx represents the layers of God's mercy in our lives.

In applying these verses, we understand that the real treasures of this earth can only be found by pursuing the glory of God and submitting to His purification process. Our spiritual food comes through prayer and intercession coupled with obedience to God's plan for our lives (see John 4:34). This type of life is a sweet fragrance before God's throne. In the end, I'm sure we will all look back in amazement and see how the entire fabric of our lives was literally woven with layers of God's grace and favor as we marched forward as overcomers.

What wonderful promises can be associated with the onyx, God's stone of overcoming grace! Still, as we progress through to spiritual maturity, there will be times when we feel as though the challenges before us are beyond our spiritual capabilities. In fact, I'm convinced that this will be true much of the time.

Yes, the challenges we face are beyond *our* capabilities, but they are never beyond the ability of God! God knows that we would never fully understand His grace unless we experienced it firsthand. So, He arranges for us to see His grace covering us as we step out in faith. Even in the midst of our many immaturities, He chooses at times to pour out His power in amazing ways!

REFLECTIONS ON THE ROCK

The truth is, He loves us! He also loves the people to whom we are ministering. And when He chooses to lavish us with His grace, all we can do is humbly receive what He desires to give us. I know the day will come when we will be privileged to look upon the fabric of our own lives and see how the grace and mercy of God were poured out time and time again.

Our only task in all this is to carefully guard our passion for God and step out in faith even when we see the challenges looming before us.

Step out in obedience and He will be there. The light He has given us will be sufficient to walk us through this spiritual training ground here on earth.

LET'S PRAY!

Lord Jesus, I come before You in thanksgiving for all the times You've showered me with Your grace and mercy. Forgive me for those times when I have not recognized Your amazing gifts and have instead taken them for granted.

Lord, I want to continue to live and move ahead in Your Kingdom and I know that only occurs when I guard my heart against becoming lukewarm. The darkness of this world is always trying to wear me out with its cares and distractions. Help me to be wise and not foolish, that I may finish the race that's set before me.

Holy Spirit, I ask You to clearly show me the areas in which I have allowed fear of the unknown or the tendency to guard my personal comfort to be the determining factors in my life decisions. (If you hear words or see pictures of areas in your life where either of these tendencies has been manifested, please take note of them.)

Lord, I ask for Your forgiveness for allowing fear or personal comfort to dictate whether or not I obey Your voice. (Specifically list the things He has shown you and ask for His forgiveness of those sins.) I lay these areas down at Your feet and ask for new grace and mercy to help me to act in obedience in the future. Please rekindle my passion for You!

In the name of Jesus, I come against all fear and desire for self-comfort and I tell you to go! All laziness and lethargy go! All disobedience must go now! I don't want you any more! Your power over me has been broken! I send you to the feet of Jesus!

Holy Spirit, I now ask that You would refill me with more of You. Fill me with renewed passion to step out in obedience. Grant me the grace to move beyond my comfort zones into realms of faith within the Kingdom of God.

Thank You, Lord, for answering this prayer. In Jesus' name. Amen.

THE LORD'S WORD TO YOU

Dearest overcomer,

My eyes have been upon you even in the midst of your darkest moments. My strength flowed through you as you submitted to My plans, though you understood very little. Your faithfulness to endure has brought about the promise of great fruitfulness and the evidences of My favor all around you. Stand strong and pursue Me with even greater fervor. The planted seed will shortly bring forth double fruit causing you to forget the anguish of the past as you're surrounded by the joys of the present.

ENDNOTES

1. Personal interview with Carla Reed.

2. Crosswalk, www. Crosswalk.com (accessed April 29, 2009).

3. James Strong, *Strong's Exhaustive Concordance,* "Deuteronomy 33:15", s.v. ancient, Strong's Hebrew # 6924, *qedem.*

4. James Strong, *Strong's Exhaustive Concordance,* "Deuteronomy 33:17," s.v. Manassah, Hebrew #4519 *Ephraim,* Hebrew #669, 3130, 3254.

5. Rings & Things, http://www.rings-things.com/gemstone/o.htm (accessed April 29, 2009).

6. Ruth V. Wright and Robert L. Chadbourne, *Crystals, Gems & Minerals of the Bible* (New Canaan, CT: Keats Publishing, Inc., 1970), 119.

7. Rings & Things, http://www.rings-things.com/gemstone/o.htm (accessed April 29, 2009).

8. *The New Strong's Exhaustive Numbers and Concordance with Expanded Greek-Hebrew Dictionary*. CD-ROM. Biblesoft, Inc., and International Bible Translators, Inc., s.v. "sardonux," (NT 4557).

9. Ibid., s.v. "gregoreuo" (NT 1127) and s.v. "egeiro" (NT 1453).

Chapter Seven
Peace While Facing Giants

CARNELIAN—REUBEN'S STONE

You were in Eden, the garden of God;
every precious stone was your covering:
*the **sardius**, topaz, and diamond, beryl,*
onyx, and jasper, sapphire, turquoise
and emerald with gold… (Ezekiel 28:13).

Nearly four years ago, Pastor Mike was a part of an intercessory group of about 30 people who all witnessed gold dust suddenly appearing on all the prayer warriors that day. The experience further inspired him to continue believing God for other physical manifestations of His glory among the people of God. So when his young son discovered a large crystal-like gemstone under their couch three days after one of his weekly home meetings, he was not surprised.

Finding a stone about the size of an egg and having witnessed many other gemstones appearing at church meetings, both he and his family recognized that this large stone had to have come from Heaven.[1]

This stone, however, was uniquely theirs, a gift from God. The gemstone reminded Pastor Mike of the gates of crystal described in Isaiah

54:12 and the glory of New Jerusalem, also pictured as crystal in the Book of Revelation. This greatly blessed him. Later, when he and several other men were asked to pray for a friend suffering from bursitis, they decided to have him hold the stone while they prayed for him. The man was instantly healed![2]

As emphasized in the beginning of this book, we absolutely realize that it is not the stone itself that brought healing to our brother, but rather an increase of faith in God inspired by this stone from Heaven.

FACING LIFE'S GIANTS

Similarly, we can look at the carnelian or sardius, a stone probably assigned to the tribe of Reuben[3] and the sixth foundational stone (see Rev. 21:20) as being representative of the peace God gives when we face the "giants" of life.

Six signifies the number of man, as he was created on the sixth day. We were God's final creation, made in His own image with the ability to reason with our intellect and having the capacity to relate to others. Most of us are able to hear, see, speak, taste, and feel. These senses grant us the opportunity to explore the world around us while we continually learn more about ourselves and our God.

The task of being fruitful and multiplying on the earth was given to man as he learned how to subdue the planet and take his God-given dominion over all living things. The Bible is full of examples of people taking their rightful positions as heirs of the Kingdom of God. The Scriptures also record the stories of those who failed to keep their eyes upon the Son and so missed their rightful calling, falling into destruction.

The name *sardius* is the ancient Greek and Roman name for a reddish precious stone. The name *Reuben* has been translated as "see or behold the son"[4] as declared by poor Leah at his birth in Genesis 29:32. She hoped this son would cause her husband to love her. Unfortunately, this was not the case. Later, Jacob called Reuben his "might" and "firstborn," but then disqualified him for an earlier sexual indiscretion (see Gen. 49:3-4). Though Jacob declared Reuben's eventual destruction, Moses reversed that curse in Deuteronomy 33:6 by saying that Reuben would live and not die.

In examining the prophetic promises given to Reuben and those who might be facing giants of their own, we are reminded of many Bible heroes who accepted the possibility of death as they looked at their great looming challenges: David confronting Goliath; Moses standing before Pharaoh; Daniel looking upon the hungry lions. In each circumstance, these heroes would have failed if they had looked merely to their own strength and abilities to face their giants. When all looked impossible, God declared that these heroes would live and not die. (See First Samuel 17; Book of Exodus; Daniel 6.)

Today we have Jesus as our intercessor assisting us in each battle. It is He who declares we will live and not die. As we behold the Son of God while facing our giants, we learn that Jesus has already given us the victory and our only challenge is to remain in His peace as we move ahead in obedience.

In further examining David and his courageous confrontation of Goliath in First Samuel 17:4-51, we see that a single stone slung in the power and authority of God was able to take down the giant. Later we find that David not only took down his giant, but was able to pass on his courageous obedience to the men who followed him. His contagious boldness encouraged his men to later take down their own giants in Second Samuel 21:19-22, where four more giants met the same fate as their brother, Goliath.

Courageous obedience is the standard established for us; we see it play out in the very humanity of the apostles and disciples. Their levels of courage and obedience alternately rose and fell during their training process under the watchful eyes of Jesus. However, the tide was turned once the power of the Holy Spirit was released upon these men in the Book of Acts. Victories came more consistently and frequently as they learned to walk by faith and not by sight. As long as they remained with their vision locked upon Jesus, they were able to overcome whatever the world threw at them.

REUBEN'S RED STONE

In studying carnelian, we learn that it is a reddish form of chalcedony, which is a variety of quartz. In its natural state, carnelian shows a cloudy distribution of its reddish color; but many of the samples today are heat-treated in order to bring out its fiery red-orange hue.

This beautiful stone has been found in royal tombs dating back to 2500 B.C. and throughout history. In 1922, the tomb of Queen Shub-ad was discovered in the Ur of Sumer (or Chaldees) region where a lush cape of polished gold decorated with carnelian, lapis lazuli, and assorted beads was wrapped around her remains.[5] Egyptian King Tutankhamen's casket was covered with turquoise, lapis lazuli, and carnelian stones.[6]

In a 3,000-year-old tomb discovered in the country of Jordan, the remains of another regal lady, possibly a queen, included a ten-foot-long necklace of 670 carnelian beads and 72 gold beads.[7]

Carnelian was a common choice for signet rings, cameos, and intaglios for the Greeks and Romans, while the Tibetans created amulets of silver with generous applications of carnelian throughout their jewelry.

In the Bible, carnelian was considered a precious stone, even in the Garden of Eden as onyx is mentioned and carnelian (or sard) is often a layer found within the onyx stone. (See Genesis 2:12.) Spiritually speaking, this stone represents our face-down with giants. It is something my husband and I have had several opportunities to practice throughout our marriage—especially in regards to our children.

GIANTS OF OUR OWN

One Sunday afternoon my husband and I were thrust from a restful afternoon into a state of high alert by the screams of one of our children outside. We could tell from his cry that something very serious had occurred. Jordan, our eight-year-old son was lying on the ground with a broken right arm, piteously declaring that it was ruined and beyond repair.

Though we assured him that the doctors would be able to fix his arm, it was an unnerving experience to look at the limb, which now looked as though it had two elbows. I felt sick at the sight of it, but tried to control my fears for the children's sakes.

Broken bones were a new experience for us as parents and his moans of excruciating pain only added to my panic. Quickly, we placed Jordan's arm on a pillow, rounded up the other three children and rushed to the hospital.

Unfortunately, my level of faith in prayer over this situation was not where it should have been. The anguish I experienced nearly caused me to faint as Jordan screamed for me to rescue him during the resetting of his bones before the cast was placed on his arm. I had to be escorted out of the office during the procedure. Finally, the arm was fixed and we were free to return home, exhausted after many long hours at the hospital.

The healing process took six weeks. However, during that time, Jordan managed to enjoy the warm summer days with his friends and siblings. He simply wrapped his cast in plastic bags and held it above his head so he could sit in the shallow pool the kids had in the backyard.

Eventually, the time came for the cast to come off; we were all jubilant to see that day arrive. Apart from looking thin and pale, Jordan's arm had healed.

Within a couple of weeks after Jordan's cast came off, one of the older boys came rushing into the house with a sobering announcement. While riding his bike in the backyard, Jordan had hit a dirt clod and toppled over sideways. Normally, this wouldn't seem like much of an incident, except that the same arm had broken again (even though we had been told that this could *not* happen due to the calcium that builds up around healed bones).

John rushed out to the back field and returned with Jordan in his arms. The same arm was broken in precisely the same location. This time, however, an evangelist who was visiting with us just happened to be sitting in our living room. Together with our guest, we prayed in agreement asking

God for a miracle. When we finished, the arm looked the same, but all the pain had suddenly vanished. A supernatural peace settled over the whole family as we prepared to visit the hospital once again.

Once there, the admitting nurse questioned us as to whether the arm was actually broken. Jordan seemed so calm, it was hard for her to imagine the child had a broken limb. However, all doubt was erased when John pulled back the towel covering the arm revealing the double-elbowed limb. The nurse had no more questions and quickly arranged for us to be admitted.

Our experience the second time was completely different from the first. Jordan required no pain medication at all as the bones were painlessly snapped back into place. Once again a cast was placed on the arm and we were sent home only a couple of hours after our arrival. We even had time to make the meeting planned for that night!

The real proof of the miracle was actually revealed six weeks later when the time came to remove the cast. After a new set of x-rays had been taken, the doctor came into the room to discuss follow-up procedures with us. While he was talking, I happened to take a closer look at both the x-ray from six weeks earlier and the recent x-ray he had displayed for us.

In the new x-ray there appeared to be three bones in the forearm, not just two bones as one would normally expect. Puzzled, I asked the doctor to explain what I was seeing.

"This is where the broken bone has healed," he said while pointing to the calcium build-up in the x-ray. Looking at the second bone in the forearm, he said that it appeared to be unbroken. Still confused, I asked him to explain the two pieces of bone appearing immediately above the unbroken bone.

"That appears to be the old broken bone," he stated, "but don't worry. It'll eventually dissolve."

"Are you telling me that there's one healed bone, one new bone and an older broken bone in our son's arm?" I questioned him. "Is that normal?"

Obviously uncomfortable, the doctor did his best to skirt the issue and left as quickly as possible. He had no natural explanation for what we saw. This was obviously a wonderful miracle of God.

In this learning experience, I had initially walked in fear; this allowed the enemy to bring additional pain and suffering in my own life. I failed the first test, but (through a series of unusual circumstances) I was better prepared eight weeks later. The second time Jordan broke his arm, we all stood up in faith and believed God for His miraculous intervention on our behalf. In boldness and the peace that passes all understanding, we stood against the "giant" and in the end the victory was the Lord's.

Many years later, we had the opportunity to face down this same giant of fear to an even greater degree. In the summer of 2001 our family was returning from a family reunion held in Lake Tahoe, California. On the way down the mountain, a truck attempting to make a left turn in front of us had for some unknown reason decided to stop his truck directly in our path as we traveled down the highway at 55 miles per hour. In an effort to avoid flipping our van, John slammed on the brakes praying that the driver would suddenly decide to hit the gas and avoid a collision.

He didn't.

The impact was hard, breaking one of our seat belts and sending both Josh and Jeremiah, our elder teenaged sons, flying forward in a heap. Josh sprained his ankle in the midst of all the mayhem. Our two younger children, Natalie and Jordan, were restrained by lap belts, but the impact caused serious visible injuries in their abdominal areas. Of the four children, only Jeremiah was uninjured.

The older van had no air bags, but miraculously the shoulder belt prevented John from hitting the steering wheel and me from going through the windshield. John had slid downward hitting the pedals with his legs. Searing pain ran through his legs, leaving him in agony. He felt as though something was broken. My knee went through the engine cover, but still in the shock from the accident, my bruised knee and chest pains from the shoulder restraints went unnoticed.

It didn't look good. Even one of the paramedics began to cry when he saw our family members laid out on the highway median in varying degrees of pain. Five of us ended up strapped down on boards and sent in two different ambulances to a local emergency room.

Jeremiah and I were able to make a couple of phone calls shortly after the accident asking family and friends to pray for us. Word went out and much prayer went up on our behalf.

Even with chaotic activity on all sides, there was a deep sense of peace that settled over our family. We were hurting; we didn't understand why this had happened, but we knew God was with us in the midst of our storm.

Later, one of the nurses in the emergency room came and asked me about our family. "I don't know what it is," she said, "but there's so much peace over all of you."

We had faced this giant before. Our eyes were on Jesus.

After the initial assessments of our injuries, Natalie and Jordan were transferred via an ambulance to a larger hospital in Roseville, California, about an hour away, for further testing and observation. They spent the night there while the rest of us were released that evening.

The following day, after a miraculous medical turnaround for the younger children, Natalie and Jordan were also released. We left with no broken bones and no serious injuries. Josh had to be on crutches for a time while nursing his sprained ankle, but that and all of our numerous bruises eventually healed.

God had intervened again on our behalf!

Though we still don't fully understand all the purposes of this accident, we understand that we have a real enemy who desires to take us out before our time. We also understand that we have a Savior who promises that He will never leave us nor forsake us (Heb. 13:5), no matter what the circumstances. Regardless of what happens to us, He will use us to touch the lives of those around us in amazing ways—if we will continue to keep our eyes on Him.

LOVE AMIDST THE TRIALS

The beautiful variations of carnelian or sardius stone can remind us of the Son of God who died and suffered on our behalf in order to give us what we need to face the many giants of this world. Yes, there will be times when we don't fully understand why it was necessary to go through various trials. However, faith is not a matter of fully understanding all that occurs in our lives; it's about keeping our eyes fixed upon the One who loves our souls with an everlasting compassion.

As we focus on the Lover of our souls, He will flood us with all we need in any given situation. He will use our circumstances to test our faith and to draw out what doesn't belong in us so that we can be refilled with even more of Him. The Lord is not so much interested in our personal comfort as He is in our personal transformation into the image of Himself.

By looking to our Savior, we can listen and learn the things He desires to teach us and take on the courageous obedience modeled by David and his mighty men when they faced down the giants.

Carnelian can remind us that all the giants of fear will eventually fall as we find our place of peaceful trust and faith in God while keeping our eyes firmly fixed upon the Lord.

REFLECTIONS ON THE ROCK

There inevitably comes a season in our lives when we find ourselves face to face with a giant. The giant screams and yells, informing us that we can never overcome him. He openly mocks us and the God we serve telling us that the moment we step out onto the battlefield, he will defeat us.

Many of us choose to behave in the same manner the tribes of Israel did while serving under King Saul. We might be on the battlefield dressed up for war and surrounded by our comrades, yet, instead of taking God's authority and facing down the giant, we might falter in faith and cower before him. We may look as though we have it all together, but on the inside, we're "freaking out." It's much easier in our own minds to ignore the problem by focusing on the peripherals rather than directly facing the assault while guarded by the peace of God.

If we stand up in faith and courage, we will find more often than not that the threats were just lies; and the giant will suddenly fall before us. Even when it appears as though the enemy has won, the ultimate victory will be God's if we hold on through the storm.

Let's Pray!

Lord, I admit that I've been afraid of the many giants I've come across in my life. At times I have chosen to ignore the battle rather than face it head on and wait for You to demonstrate Your power in my life. I've given in to fear and panic rather than trusting You in all circumstances. Please forgive me for my lack of faith in You.

Holy Spirit, I ask that You would show me any areas in which I have avoided the battles rather than moving out in faith and realizing the victory I have through You. (As you see pictures or words in your mind, write them down.)

Jesus, I ask for Your forgiveness for (name the situation or offense). I chose to avoid the battle rather than defeat my giants. I realize that I was focusing more on them than on You, the God of giant-killers. Please wash me in Your blood that I might be released from all fear and guilt.

In the name of Jesus, I come against all spirits associated with (name the situation or offense). I tell you that you no longer have any influence in my life! Your power has been broken and I send you to the feet of Jesus! Go now!

Holy Spirit, I now ask that You would come and strengthen my courage. Grant me all I need to become a giant-killer. Fill me with Your peace, especially when I am in the midst of storms. Help me to live and walk in faith and not in fear. In Jesus' name I ask this. Amen.

THE LORD'S WORD TO YOU

Dear giant-slayer,

Even as you stand before your giants of life, think back to the many battles we've previously walked through together. Did I ever forsake you? Never! Neither will I abandon you during your time of need. Don't let the fiery furnace before you or the circling lions around you shake your faith. Keep your eyes on Me, not your circumstances. Remember, neither the battle nor the victory necessarily look the way you might have expected them to look. You might not even understand the purposes of these challenges. Just rest in My peace. Trust in My strength. Focus on My love for you.

If you will take the first step, you'll find My presence is with you. Together we shall take down your giant and you will emerge the victor, with even greater authority.

ENDNOTES

1. Personal interview, April 2008, confirmed by two other people.

2. The stone and tribe of Naphtali came together through the process of elimination. The meaning of both the name and the seventh position convinced me that these two belonged together. There is some speculation involved in this process as mentioned in the *Jewish Encyclopedia,* http://www.jewish encyclopedia.com/view.jsp?artid=1433&letter=B&search= breastplate%20stones (accessed May 4, 2009).

2. Personal interview, April 2008.

3. Rings & Things, http://www.rings-things.com/gemstone/c.htm.

4. *The Strong's New Exhaustive Numbers and Concordance with Expanded Greek-Hebrew Dictionary.* CD-ROM. Biblesoft, Inc., and International Bible Translators, Inc., s.v. "Re'uwben," (OT 7205).

5. Ruth V. Wright and Robert L. Chadbourne, *Crystals, Gems & Minerals of the Bible* (New Canaan, CT: Keats Publishing, Inc., 1970), 31.

6. Ibid.

7. Ibid., 30.

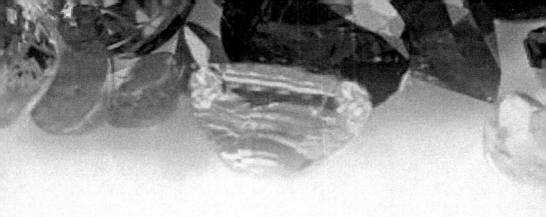

Chapter Eight
Falling on the Rock

DIAMOND/ROCK CRYSTAL/CHRYSOLITE—NAPHTALI'S STONE

*... The fifth sardonyx, the sixth sardius,
the seventh **chrysolite...** (Revelation 21:20).*

For Terrie, it was not unlike any other morning on which she woke up early to get ready for work. She quickly dressed, ate, and then prepared to read a little in her Bible before heading out the door.

As she cracked open the well-worn pages of her father's old Bible, she noticed an unusual bump. Carefully, she turned each page until she came to the source. Her eyes widened in amazement as she discovered ten to fifteen perfectly cut diamond-like gemstones all lying in a row along the binding of the book. She immediately noticed a sweet fragrance emanating from the pages.

Inspecting the book more closely, she found that only certain verses on those pages were clearly highlighted with something she refers to as "diamond dust." The pearly sheen was seen on specific verses the Lord obviously wanted to draw attention to both in her life and in the lives of those with whom she shared this blessing.

As this amazing phenomena continued (and still continues to this day!) at random times, Terrie has found highlighted verses such as Matthew 19:23-24, Matthew 20:1-16, and First Corinthians 2:1-5.

The diamond-like gemstones found within the pages were carefully placed in small bags and taken to church services where Terrie and her husband would pass out these "seed gemstones" as directed by the Holy Spirit.

Though at times they would have distributed all the gemstones they had, more diamond-like gemstones would always appear, either in Terrie's Bible or in the bags carrying the gemstones. It seemed that as long as they faithfully gave as God directed, their supply never ran out.[1]

Just as the Lord used these diamond-like gemstones and "diamond dust" to highlight His truths to Terrie, so in the same manner, the beautiful clarity of the diamond or chrysolite stone can speak of clearness in the Spirit of God. As Naphtali's stone, from the definition of his name, we can see a picture of the wrestling and intertwining of ourselves with our God as we discover the joy that comes when we willingly die to our own ways and yield to the Lover of our souls.[2]

As the seventh stone which indicates completion or perfection, I came to understand that this stage represents a completion of our *wrestling* with God. I am reminded of Jacob wrestling with "a man" (see Gen. 32:24-30). In the end, he was left "crippled" and yet greatly blessed by God. I believe the Lord wants us to be mindful of our own weakness, so He can show Himself mighty through us.

Like a deer let loose from its captors, Jacob describes Naphtali as both a deer and one who uses beautiful words (see Gen. 49:21). This diamond stage speaks of one who has learned to use his God-given authority appropriately. He speaks life and not death to those around him.

Later, in Deuteronomy 33:23, Moses proclaimed Naphtali as one who has been filled and satisfied with the pleasures of God. The opportunity is given for those in this stage to take possession of the "west" and the "south." By looking again at the symbolism of the four winds mentioned in chapter five, we see that Naphtali's diamond stage grants us the privilege of using God's authority to halt assaults against us while experiencing seasons of rapid growth in the Kingdom of God.

THE SEVENTH STONE

Learning the identity of this seventh stone and its relationship to Israel's 12 tribes was a bit challenging as Christian and Jewish scholars alike seem to disagree as to the stone's actual identification. *Diamond,* the word used in Exodus 28:18 is almost assuredly not referring to diamonds as we know them today. Diamonds had not yet been discovered nor cut until much later in history.[2] Some scholars say that rock crystal, a clear variety of quartz, would more likely be the stone they were using at the time.

Another challenge in determining the stone's identity is the fact that chrysolite, a yellowish variety of peridot mentioned in Revelation 21, was thought to be possibly topaz. Yet, topaz is mentioned later as the ninth foundation stone. In researching this, I found that both chrysolite and rock crystal are varieties of quartz. By examining the symbolism of the seventh position and the definition of Naphtali's name, I found some striking similarities.

The word *chrysolite* is translated as "gold-stone," a "yellow gem" or a "stumbling stone"[3] and has roots going far back into history. Pliny the Elder, author of *Naturalis Historia* ("Natural History"), mentioned in this A.D. 70 book that Saint John's Island in the Red Sea is a deposit of chrysolite. To this day Saint John's Island is still producing this gemstone. Legends state that chrysolite was a favorite of Cleopatra and that some of the "emeralds" she wore were actually peridot, a green variety of chrysolite.[4]

Pliny stated that chrysolite was first discovered by pirates driven to St. John's Island by adverse winds. Legend has it that the inhabitants of that island used to pay tribute to the Egyptian rulers using chrysolite as their currency. Apparently the islanders thought that chrysolite could only be found at night as the stones supposedly "glowed like the sun."[5]

The gem seekers would mark the location of the stones at night, but believed chrysolite could only be retrieved during the daylight hours.

Interestingly enough, chrysolite, which is an old name for peridot, is also occasionally found embedded in meteorites.[6]

I'm not sure about the significance of chrysolite's presence on meteorites; but I believe it is possible that God simply takes pleasure in astounding us. This may be just another reminder of the fact that the same Creator who created the earth also created the heavens.

WHAT ABOUT "SEVEN"?

Seven, an important number throughout the Bible, represents completion and is a metaphor of Christ Himself. Seven days of creation were mentioned in Genesis. Revelation tells us that there were seven churches, seven lamp stands, and seven stars in John's prophetic vision. Seven angels sound seven trumpets in Revelation 8 while the mysterious seven thunders in Revelation 10 signal the finality of God's judgments upon the earth.

So, what role does the number *seven* portray in helping us better understand our growth in the Kingdom of God?

By looking at the life of Jesus as our example, we can see that completing God's plan for our lives leads not only to the fulfillment of His will, but also the death of our flesh. When Jesus accomplished His literal death on the cross, He declared, *"It is finished!"* (John 19:30). Jesus had completed His Father's purpose on earth. He had been emptied and hollowed out of all self-will. He willingly laid down His life into the hands of His Father and was resurrected three days later.

It's interesting to note that both rock crystal and chrysolite are somewhat transparent stones that have little or no color. The Hebrew word used in Exodus for "diamond" is *y'aahalom,*[7] which comes from the root *halam,* whose meaning has to do with hardness and means to "strike down," "hammer," or "conquer."[8]

As a very hard stone used to drill through dense materials, I can see the seventh stage, spiritually speaking, as being a time in which I come to the end of myself—a season of falling on the Rock so that He does not have to fall on me (Matt. 21:44). It is the day when His will has finally overcome my own.

The name *Naphtali* means "wrestling, to twine, to struggle."[9] From what I've seen in my own life, it's the nature of humankind to wrestle with God over the release of control over their lives and destinies. It's amazing to think that we struggle over this control and imagine that our own wills are better than what the Creator might plan for us. Yet, that's exactly what we do.

A Memorable Wrestling Match

I can still remember the first time a challenge came to my plans for my life. As both a child and teenager, I struggled with deep feelings of inferiority and fear; they crippled my early life in many ways, despite the fact that I recognized the problem.

Prior to giving my life to Jesus, I had pushed myself to be a part of the drama department in our high school. It was part of my effort to overcome my fears. The attention I received by being on stage helped me to overcome my poor self-image, because I was at least temporarily able to become someone else.

After several years of training and experience, I determined that I wanted to become an actress as an adult. When I met Jesus as my Savior, many things changed rapidly in my life. Drama, however, was not something I was initially willing to lay down and yield to God. I still wanted to become an actress, but now I desired to become a Christian actress.

That summer I had an opportunity to attend a Christian camp for young people. The worship and instruction offered at the camp were both inspiring and challenging. Everything was going along fine until one of the counselors and I started discussing my plans for the future. Excitedly, I described all that I had planned for the years ahead. After listening patiently, he asked me one simple question; it bothered me for days.

"Have you ever asked the Lord about His plans for your life?" he challenged.

Reluctantly, I admitted that I hadn't.

"Don't you think you should find out what He has in mind for you?"

The questions grew harder and harder. I didn't want to let go of this part of my life. I enjoyed acting. I had already invested quite of bit of time in the field of drama. Was I willing to lay all that down? Not really. But I did agree to pray about it.

It took many days for me to work up the courage to even ask the Lord about this issue. When I finally did pray, I spoke honestly about my feelings and all the starry-eyed dreams I had envisioned for the future before I laid all of them down at His feet.

His answer didn't come immediately, so I assumed that I could just go on with my plans. That fall, I re-entered drama classes at my high school and did my best to participate ... but something had changed. The passion I felt previously was greatly diminished. Nothing about drama appealed to me any longer. I began seeing this class as a waste of my time and energy. Shortly after meeting with my school counselor, I transferred into a journalism class that really served me well in preparation for all the writing I've done since that time.

Looking back, I now see my wrestling with God as a great blessing. Little by little, He challenged me to lay everything down before Him. Bit by bit, He continues working on me; He is helping me to release every expectation and claim to entitlement I once believed was indispensable or rightfully mine.

ROOTING OUT "ENTITLEMENT"

So many times we think that if we go to church or spend time in prayer, we have "earned" the right to pamper our flesh in some area.

We think we are "entitled" to feed our fleshly cravings. Recently, I discovered an area of entitlement in my own life that really surprised me, as I thought I had already laid down this area of my life.

When my husband and I moved to Washington State, we both began searching for jobs to help pay off moving expenses and keep up with living expenses. I was eventually hired as a substitute interpreter for the deaf with a local school district. The problem was that this job was much more mentally taxing than I had anticipated. Additional drawbacks were the early morning calls that came Mondays through Fridays, asking me to show up at whichever school needed me.

My flesh hated it!

One evening, the battle was so intense that I didn't want to turn on my phone; I simply didn't want to work the next day. My husband immediately spotted my spiritual battle and challenged me on it. (Bless his heart!) I didn't want to hear about it and then fought feelings of rebellion as he instructed me to turn on the phone in case a job came in. Reluctantly, I complied…and a call for a job did come in.

Several days later, the Holy Spirit finally revealed the root entitlements I had been struggling with. Some time back, I had convinced myself that because I was "older," I shouldn't have to work any kind of difficult job; I felt I *deserved* to sleep in some mornings.

Very gently, the Holy Spirit laid these lies before me and asked me whether or not I had truly laid down my life as a living sacrifice. It was obvious from all my grumbling and complaining that I had not. After a time of true repentance before the Lord, He granted me the grace to do whatever I needed to do for that season of our lives.

Although I try to be sensitive to the Holy Spirit, I am far from perfect. I am sure that, in the days and years ahead, there will be other areas of fleshly entitlement uncovered by the Holy Spirit. I am confident that He will gently highlight those weaknesses and grant me the grace to repent and deal with them. Layer by layer, I am being hollowed out so more of God's glory can reside within me. As I die to my fleshly desires,

I am allowing my increasing spiritual clarity to reflect more and more of the glory of the Lord.

I'm certain that when the Lord sees a vessel that's been hollowed and poured out, He rejoices knowing there is yet another person who can be filled to overflowing with His presence.

The world thought that when Jesus died, it was all over, but the best was yet to come! The resurrected Jesus prepared His disciples for the next wave of glory that came in an astonishing way when the Holy Spirit was first released on the earth. Likewise, I believe that diamonds, rock crystal, and chrysolite can remind us of these principles.

Each of us, as we surrender, can begin to truly reflect the many facets of God's character demonstrated by His love flowing out of us. The less of *self* we hang on to, the more we reflect His glory to others—just as a diamond reflects the colors of the rainbow when light hits the stone.

REFLECTIONS ON THE ROCK

When honestly examining our naturally rebellious and selfish ways, the difficulty of laying it all down at Jesus' feet can seem overwhelming. Yet, this is what it means to crucify our flesh daily. The goal for each of us is to become so transparent that only the loving character of Jesus shows through 24 hours a day—and not just when we're in front of others!

One scheme of the enemy is to convince us that we *deserve* something, so that when we're denied that particular *entitlement* we become upset and look for ways to blame others for our loss. If we work to surrender all of our expectations to God, we can genuinely appreciate His blessing the way He wants us to.

Our flesh wants to excuse bad behavior by reasoning that we were just tired and couldn't help ourselves. Our minds want to blame others for "forcing" us to act and react poorly. None of our excuses hold water; not even the excuse of being born with a certain personality type or temperament based on our nationality or family line. If our personality, thoughts, or behaviors conflict with the nature of Jesus, it's sin, plain and simple. When our sin nature causes us to stumble repeatedly in the same area, we must discover the root of that sin, repent of it, and cast it out immediately.

Jesus warned us that whoever falls on the Rock (Jesus) will be broken and humbled, but those who choose to ignore Him will be crushed. Listen to His words from Matthew 21:44: *"Whoever falls on this stone will be broken; but on whomever it falls, it will grind him to powder."*

His efforts in teaching us true humility will only increase according to our need to learn. This verse alone is enough to encourage all of us to agree with God in His transformation plans.

Let's Pray!

Lord Jesus, I choose to humble myself before You. I lay my life, hopes, dreams, and plans before You. I even surrender what I consider to be my ministry here on earth. I empty myself of all I know and I choose to agree with You that Your understanding far outweighs my knowledge or understanding.

I pour out my life as a drink offering before You. I no longer want to cling to my old behaviors or ways of thinking. I give them all to You and give You permission to transform me totally into Your image. This life is not mine, but Yours. Do with me as You wish.

Holy Spirit, I ask You to examine the depths of who I am and show me every area that I have yet to yield. Turn on the searchlight and reveal any sources of pride lurking within so that I may humble myself before God. (Listen to what He says.)

Lord Jesus, I ask that You forgive me for (name the offense). Forgive me for any areas of control to which I still cling. Wash me now in Your blood that I might be clean in Your sight. I no longer want to resist You in any way.

In the name of Jesus, I come against (name any source of resistance) that has resisted the plan of God in my life. All control, I don't want you any more. I remind you that you were defeated

2,000 years ago! You have lost your foothold in my life! I cast you away and send you to the feet of Jesus! Leave now!

Lord I ask that You fill me with humility. I bow before You, the Rock of my salvation in full surrender. Thank You for hearing and answering my prayers. In Jesus' name. Amen.

THE LORD'S WORD TO YOU

Dearest possessor of My authority,

Your new freedom brings Me great joy as I watch you run like a deer released from its enclosure. Take my gifts and use them as My Spirit directs. You've learned much from past battles and now your yielding has brought some of what I have in store for you. Use this time wisely. Draw closer to Me than ever before as I am a deep well of experiences and learning. This is only the beginning of our adventure into realms of increasing revelation of who I AM and who you are to become. As old things are driven out, be saturated with Me. My love awaits you.

ENDNOTES

1. Personal interview, April 2008, and continuing experience as I've continued regular phone contact with them.

2. Ruth V. Wright and Robert L. Chadbourne, *Crystals, Gems & Minerals of the Bible* (New Canaan, CT: Keats Publishing, Inc., 1970), 55; *The Zondervan Pictorial Bible Dictionary* (Grand Rapids, MI: Zondervan) 537.

3. *The New Strong's Exhaustive Numbers and Concordance with Expanded Greek-Hebrew Dictionary.* CD-ROM. Biblesoft, Inc., and International Bible Translators, Inc., s.v. "chrusolithos" (NT 5555) and s.v. "lithos" (NT 3037).

4. Bernardine Fine Art Jewelry, "Peridot Facts, Information and Description, http://www.bernardine.com/gemstones/peridot .htm (accessed May 4, 2009).

5. Ruth V. Wright and Robert L. Chadbourne, *Crystals, Gems & Minerals of the Bible* (New Canaan, CT: Keats Publishing, Inc., 1970), 37.

6. Bernardine Fine Art Jewelry, http://www.bernardine .com/gemstones/peridot.htm (accessed May 4, 2009).

7. *The New Strong's Exhaustive Numbers and Concordance with Expanded Greek-Hebrew Dictionary.* CD-ROM. Biblesoft, Inc., and International Bible Translators, Inc., s.v. "y'aaha-lam," (OT 3095).

8. Ibid., s.v. "halam," (OT 1986).

9. James Strong, *Strong's Exhaustive Concordance*, Hebrew *Naphtali* – 5321, 6617.

Chapter Nine
A Day of New Beginnings

BERYL/CHRYSOBERYL—ZEBULUN'S STONE

*... The fifth sardonyx, the sixth sardius,
the seventh chrysolite, the eighth* **beryl***...*
(Revelation 21:20).

One morning Terrie awoke to find her entire carpet strewn with small gemstones in a variety of colors. In her excitement she called her friend Carol in Spokane, Washington, to share the news of her discovery. Both she and Carol rejoiced in this new manifestation of God's love.

Sometime later Terrie and her husband came to Spokane for a ministry trip and stayed with Carol and her husband for the duration of their visit. One evening after ministering, the two couples returned to the house and walked into the living room. With the dim stove light shining in the next room, they could see the Aztec-style rug on the floor sparkling like stars in the night sky.

Excitedly, they turned on the lights and discovered an array of pink, blue, green, red, purple, orange, yellow, and clear diamond-like gemstones flashing brilliantly before them. For a moment, the two couples stood in awe at this lavish outpouring of His love upon them.

It wasn't long before the two women dropped to their hands and knees and began scooping up their sparkling treasures while laughing gleefully like children on an Easter egg hunt! Carefully, they picked up the gemstones, working to clear sections of the carpet one by one. However, it seemed that as they picked up the gemstones, more would appear. It took quite a while, but eventually they were able to complete their gathering. That evening alone, they counted 168 stones![1]

Another time on the dawn of her birthday, Terrie got up as usual to go to work. Once dressed, she came out into the living room. She headed toward her favorite armchair and turned on the light. There sitting on the armrest was a heart-shaped heliodor, which is best described as a yellow beryl gemstone. Immediately, she knew it was God's birthday present for her: another morning surprise!

Just as the light of the rising sun brings with it a revelation of God's new mercies and love, beryl and chrysoberyl can represent a new era, spiritually speaking (as they did in the case of Terrie and Carol). As the eighth foundational stone (I believe) was assigned to Zebulun, we find in beryl and chrysoberyl the promise of new beginnings and the establishment of a spiritual dowry or endowment. This will be further explained later in this chapter.

ZEBULUN'S ROCK

In Genesis 49:13, Jacob stated that Zebulun is a haven of safety for others finding refuge within his borders. Moses declared later in Deuteronomy 33:18 that Zebulun was to rejoice in all of his *"going out."* This verse also literally says that Issachar is in his tent. This indicates that all the promises made to Issachar, the final stages of our maturity, can be accessed through intimacy with the Lord. This verse promises that He will bring a reward and lift our burdens even prior to arriving at the twelfth stage of development! New avenues of ministry to the people will open up as He calls people—through us—to the mountain of God. Isn't that amazing?

To better understand more about the stone of beryl, we look to a description from Daniel 10:5-6:

> *I lifted my eyes and looked, and behold, a certain man clothed in linen, whose waist was girded with gold of Uphaz! His body was like beryl, his face like the appearance of lightning, his eyes like torches of fire, his arms and feet like burnished bronze in color, and the sound of his words like the voice of a multitude.*

From this glorious description of an angelic being recorded by Daniel, it's obvious that beryl had to be a magnificent yellow stone; however, today's scholars can only make educated guesses as to which stone this passage describes. All that is known for certain is that this particular gemstone originated from the city of Tarshish,[2] a large trading port in Old Testament times.

Today the word *beryl* refers to a large family of precious stones including emerald, aquamarine, alexandrite, and chrysoberyl. Of all the many stones falling into this category, chrysoberyl, an ancient variety, appears to fit the biblical descriptions. Today, most chrysoberyl is recovered from river sands and gravels.

Historical accounts of uses for beryl include a powdered mixture used to treat eye injuries and disorders of the heart and spine. The Egyptians of old attributed to beryl the ability to make its wearer amiable, fearless, and victorious in whatever battles they faced. Ancient gravesites located by the Nile have yielded beryl beads confirming their value to the Egyptians.[3]

During Moses' final prayer for the 12 tribes of Israel in Deuteronomy 33:18-19, both Zebulun and Issachar are mentioned together. Moses said that the two tribes *"shall partake of the abundance of the seas and of treasures hidden in the sand."* As we read earlier, chrysoberyl is found among river sands and gravels. According to Kevin Conner, author of *Interpreting the*

Symbols and Types, the sea is a symbol of the unsaved masses and sand is a symbol of Abraham's earthly seed.[4]

Proverbs 13:22 indicates that the wealth of sinners is laid up for the righteous. As we apply these various biblical truths, we find that two sources will provide the abundance spoken of in Deuteronomy 33:18-19. One source will be the unsaved masses (the seas) and the other will be Abraham's seed or people of faith (the sand). With this understanding, we can move out with great confidence to conquer new territories for the Kingdom of God and watch as God provides abundantly for all our needs.

Chrysoberyl's position as the eighth stone is also significant in that *eight* is seen as the number of resurrection. Throughout Scripture, we can see a number of "eights" replayed for us Eight people were saved in Noah's ark (see 1 Pet. 3:20). Firstborn sons were to be dedicated to the Lord (see Exod. 22:29) and circumcised on the eighth day (see Gen. 17:12). Jesus appeared eight days after his resurrection (see Matt. 28:1 and John 20:26).

The Hebrew word from which the name *Zebulun* is derived is *zabal,* which means "to inclose, to reside, to dwell with."[5] By applying all of these meanings to the stone, we can see that this stage in the believer's life is a time of spiritual resurrection that follows the "hollowing out" of the previous stage.

When we have emptied ourselves of all we are and laid it on the altar, the Lord is able to fill our empty vessels with His power. He encloses us with Himself spiritually, and the Holy Spirit resides in us to direct our steps.

GOD'S POWER IN US

At this eighth or chrysoberyl stage of spiritual growth, the hindrances of the flesh have been greatly diminished. It is not something I am claiming to have attained, but I am pressing forward to this upward calling as I learn to serve, bless, and encourage others by the life I live (see Phil. 3:14).

Some have already learned the secret of dying to their flesh and allowing the power of God to manifest through them. My husband and I have had our better moments—what I'd call a foretaste of things to come in our own lives and the lives of many other believers. Those tastes of both His presence and power have only served to stir up an even greater hunger for the Lord and all He is.

One such example occurred while we were living in Minnesota. Warmer spring air from the south was colliding with colder northern temperatures and many of us were caught in this battle of climates. A tornado watch was in place, so while staying with my sister, our families hung out in her basement. We kept one eye on the T.V.; the media flashed reports of tornado sightings all around us. Because tornado warnings are so commonplace at that time of the year, both our husbands had decided to go to work that day.

The children were hungry, so we decided to go upstairs briefly to prepare lunch for them. While we were upstairs, we glanced out the living room window and spotted a tornado forming, its thin, dark tail beginning to drop down from the clouds. I suddenly realized that this tornado would be touching down in the approximate area where my husband was probably driving!

Without thinking, I felt an authority come over me that I had never experienced before. Pointing directly at the funnel cloud, I declared that this tornado would not touch the ground. I told it to go back into the clouds from whence it came. The moment I spoke those words, the funnel cloud retreated into the clouds as quickly as it had come. My sister and I were both amazed; and only in recent years did I discover that Josh, our oldest son, had followed us up the stairs and witnessed the tornado's retreat.

As strange as it seems for human beings to be walking in that kind of authority, this is exactly the model Jesus gave us as He walked on the earth. In Mark 4:35-41, Jesus rebuked the storm and the seas became calm. In Luke 10:19, we are told that God has given us all power and authority over the enemy so that nothing can hurt us. It's up to us to learn how to walk in His authority continually.

Using our God-given authority can be the difference between life and death. One evening, just as my husband was returning home, he noticed two men involved in an altercation. It appeared that one man was pointing something at the other man, who happened to be our neighbor. As my husband got out of the car, the authority of the Lord came over him and he approached the men.

"What's going on here?" he inquired. Our neighbor quickly explained the circumstances, just as John realized that the other man had a gun in his hand. Turning around, my husband pointed his finger at the man with the gun and declared that there would be no shooting in this neighborhood.

"I bind you spirit of murder!" John declared. "We've claimed this neighborhood for Jesus Christ." The man with the gun suddenly lowered his weapon and began telling John what our neighbor had done to upset him.

"If you need to settle something," my husband continued, "you'll have to do that outside this area!" The two men obediently walked outside the perimeters of our neighborhood and quietly discussed their dispute.

John came into the house and called the police just as a precaution, but the event was over long before the police ever showed up. The authority of God came over my husband, causing him to step into a potentially dangerous situation. At least one life was spared—and maybe two. That night, my husband's obedience allowed God's authority to reign in our neighborhood.

As yielded vessels, the potential increases for a greater release of God's resurrection power to be manifested through our lives. Both beryl and chrysoberyl can remind us of the resurrected life we now live. The golden glow of the stone is reminiscent of the refining process of gold itself.

Through the fires of dying to self, our living sacrifices will eventually become a sweet fragrance in the nostrils of God.

New authority and discovery of the many treasures placed within us are the hallmarks of this chrysoberyl stage in the believer's life. Our confidence grows as we step out and bless the sea of humanity around us. Their needs will present each of us with opportunities to demonstrate both the authority and love of the Father.

REFLECTIONS ON THE ROCK

The idea of stepping out of our natural ways of living and into a supernatural way of life can seem daunting or even impossible at first. However, once we've yielded our wills to God, we can be certain that He will provide whatever skills we need for the work He has laid out before us. If we withhold nothing from Him, He will withhold nothing from us. We're able to walk in the "giving and receiving" flow found within the Kingdom of God.

This stage can be a very surprising and exciting one as we learn to abide in the Spirit and allow God to flow through us unhindered. Many times, we discover that God's methods of fulfilling promises in our lives are completely different from what we had imagined. His ways are definitely not our ways—His ways are so much better!

Though we may face new and difficult challenges in this stage, the joy and fulfillment we experience will more than make up for them. Our faith will grow in leaps and bounds as we see God do things that we had never before imagined. What a blessed time!

LET'S PRAY!

Lord Jesus, I thank You for the new levels of faith and authority that You have promised me as I move in obedience to all that You lay out before me. Help me to continually guard my heart against all the forms of spiritual pride that may try to slip in. I know that all gifts and abilities are from You and I give You all the glory for what You're doing in me and through me. Help me to stay in this guarded place of utter dependence upon You and help me to develop an ever greater love and appreciation for the Body of Christ.

Holy Spirit, I now ask You to search me again for anything that seeks to hinder the work of God in my life. Show me how I can better fulfill the purposes of God in all I say and do. (Listen to what the Holy Spirit says and then integrate His leadings into your prayer.)

Father, forgive me for (name the offense). I repent of this sin and ask for Your forgiveness. I don't want to walk in any kind of pride or self-will, but want to remain humble and broken before You. Please grant me Your grace to finish the course before me.

In the name of Jesus, I come against you spirits behind (name the offense/behavior). I tell you that you are defeated and have no more power over me in this area! I send you to the feet of Jesus! Leave me now!

Thank You, Lord Jesus, for Your amazing goodness and grace! I need You so much! You are so good! Amen.

THE LORD'S WORD TO YOU

Dear child of intimacy,

You have learned the secrets of residing in My presence. The treasures you have discovered there have helped to equip you for this season of new beginnings. Those who are hungry are drawn to the treasures of glory you bear. But there is more for you! Come search and learn of Me. Your reward already awaits you as you continue to draw closer to bask in My love.

ENDNOTES

1. Telephone interview, April 2008; confirmed by three other people.

2. *Strong's Exhaustive Concordance,* Hebrew Tarshiyah – 8659.

3. Ruth V. Wright and Robert L. Chadbourne, *Crystals, Gems & Minerals of the Bible* (New Canaan, CT: Keats Publishing, Inc., 1970), 19.

4. Kevin J. Conner, *Interpreting the Symbols and Types* (Portland, OR: City Christian Publishing), 165-166.

5. *The New Strong's Exhaustive Numbers and Concordance with Expanded Greek-Hebrew Dictionary*. CD-ROM. Biblesoft, Inc., and International Bible Translators, Inc., s.v. "zabal," (OT 2082).

Chapter Ten
Obedience Regardless of the Cost

TOPAZ—SIMEON'S STONE

… For the price of wisdom is above rubies.
*The **topaz** of Ethiopia cannot equal it,*
nor can it be valued in pure gold (Job 28:18-19).

J ames, a successful businessman from Spanaway, Washington and his wife, Jill, felt directed by the Holy Spirit to join a group of intercessors from several continents who planned to pray over specific parts of Israel while touring the Holy Land.

They were not prepared for some of the amazing encounters with the Lord they would experience during their ten-day trip. One incident, in particular, occurred as they were driving from Jerusalem through some mountainous and arid regions of Israel. Huge stones and erratically-shaped boulders lay scattered across the landscape as the rugged hills raced past them during their four-hour journey.

While the other passengers in the car slept, James meditated on the things they'd seen in God's promised land. He also pondered the numerous Old Testament verses that described the land as "flowing with milk and honey."

Puzzled by all the rocks, James decided to ask the Lord about His purpose for them. No sooner had James asked the question that the Lord responded: He said the rocks were there to sing His praises at all times. This was God's purpose in placing them where He did (see Luke 19:40).

Amazed by the Lord's answer, James took some time to consider verses in the Bible declaring that all of creation offered praise to the Creator. In childlike faith, James asked one more thing of the Lord.

"Can *I* hear the rocks sing Your praises?"

Seconds later, God opened his ears and allowed James to hear.

As he drove past the boulders around him, he heard sounds that he had never heard before. The rocks themselves were singing in chorus with brass or trumpet-like voices in an unknown language that reminded him of the Hebrew language!

"What are they saying, Lord?" James inquired.

"They are magnifying My name and declaring My praises and glory."

At one point during this song of the stones, James spotted a deep crevice between huge boulders and was able to hear the trumpet-like voices of the rocks buried deep in the earth! The song of the stones persisted for 15 amazing minutes as he continued driving down the Israeli road.

The impact of this encounter was clearly written on James's face as he described the sounds emanating from the rocks and boulders he saw in Israel's desert that day. His faith and passion for both the Creator and creation has been forever altered by his radical experience (which has also prompted an even more radical step of faith in the lives of this family).[1]

They will never be the same.

The skeptic in some of us might be tempted to question this and other supernatural acts of God. When God speaks to our hearts and reveals the treasures of Heaven, will we hesitate in unbelief or accept His gifts with childlike wonder? Will we walk in immediate obedience to the voice of our sweet Shepherd when He leads us in new paths?

THE NINTH STAGE OF MATURITY

The topaz or ninth stage of maturity in the Kingdom of God will bring us to the place where all doubt and unbelief have been rooted out of our thinking. One whose faith is purified in this way might be able to enjoy the sounds of worship emanating, not only from the stones, but possibly from the trees or flowers as well!

In further examining the significance of the number *nine,* we find Jesus completing His sacrifice on the cross during the ninth hour. Throughout the three hours of darkness that hung over the land and in spite of His intense suffering, Jesus continued to reveal the character of God. The fruit of God's Spirit was made obvious as Jesus continued to offer forgiveness and love to those around Him, causing even the most hardened of soldiers to admit that Jesus had to be the Son of God (see Matt. 27:54).

Paul also heard and understood the call of God upon his life. In fact, he knew from the very beginning that God was calling him to learn how to suffer many things for the sake of the Lord (see Acts 9:15-16). I'm sure these words were not thrilling to hear, but as Paul drew near to the Lord, a transformation began in his heart. The old man and his desires for comfort died within him. By the time Paul set out on his missionary journeys, the character of God had settled deep within him to where the apostle was able to rejoice *always,* even in his many tribulations (see Phil. 4:4).

In Second Corinthians 11:23-25, Paul ran through a list of things he had endured while following the will of God for his life: beatings, stonings, shipwreck, perilous journeys, weariness, hard work, sleeplessness, hunger, thirst, fastings, cold, and concern for all the churches. In the natural, none of it sounds the least bit appealing.

To my mind, the depth of Paul's love and devotion to God's will were most evident toward the end of his missionary journeys. It was then that he was informed repeatedly that chains and tribulation awaited him in Jerusalem. Though his friends pleaded with him not to go, Paul had heard from God and knew that his destiny lay ahead of him in Jerusalem (see

Acts 20:18-38). Fear of the unknown did not change his resolute obedience to the voice of God. His passion was only to obey God and endure whatever hardships proved to be part of that call.

We can be assured that, with God at the helm of our lives, we are moving in spiritual growth; there is nothing to fear. God has been faithful in the past and will be equally faithful in the future.

The topaz and its probable assignment to the tribe of Simeon, according to *John Gill's Exposition of the Bible,* may represent a confidence that our faith in God has been absolutely settled in our hearts.[2] Though the directives issued by the Holy Spirit may seem daunting, we are committed to following through, whatever personal cost we may face. The promise of God is that our obedience will be rewarded.

In the history of the tribe of Simeon, we once again see the important principle of adoption being played out as this tribe was eventually absorbed into the tribe of Judah. As foretold in Genesis 49:5-7, it was Simeon's violent temper that brought about these changes. This prophetic word was fulfilled in Joshua 19:9.

Fortunately, because of this new placement, the tribe of Simeon would be entitled to the promises made to Judah—the promises of great joy and great victory as Judah's hands were used both to cast out the things of the enemy and to extend upward in worship to God. These weapons became an important part of this warrior's strategy as walls of resistance crumbled before him.

The original Greek word *topazion* simply indicates a gemstone, possibly a topaz or chrysolite.[3] Other sources indicate the name for this stone was derived from the Saskrit word *tapas* meaning "fire" or the Greek word *topazos* or *topazion*, meaning "to seek". The name of *Simeon* specifically translates as "to hear intelligently (often with the implication of attention, obedience, etc.)"; "to tell."[4] These definitions indicate that both the gifts and the fruit of the Spirit are in operation. The stone's position as the ninth foundation stone represents finality, fullness, fruitfulness, the number of the Holy Spirit, and fruit of the womb. Again, at this ninth stage, we can see a confidence and maturity demonstrated by our ability to hear the voice of the Lord and walk in the fullness of the Holy Spirit.

Putting all of this together, we find that the topaz could represent a level of maturity in the Spirit at which the believer would no longer find himself or herself questioning the Lord's directives. It is the stage for which radical obedience is a trademark.

THE TOPAZ IN HISTORY

In examining the history of the topaz, we find that it has been regarded as a gemstone for at least 2,000 years. Though no one is sure of the size or quality of the *"topaz of Ethiopia"* mentioned in Job 28:19, it's obvious that this must have been a magnificent stone. However, we are told that the wisdom of God far outweighs it in value.

Some ancient records embellish on the imaginary powers of the topaz, including its alleged ability to prevent sudden death and improve vision. The assertion that seems to top them all is the claim that, if a topaz were dropped into a pot of boiling water, a person could retrieve it with their bare hands—and suffer no harm![5] In biblical tradition, it was thought that topaz, the ninth foundation stone in Revelation 21, could serve as protection against one's enemies and stand as a symbol of both beauty and splendor.

One ancient legend speaks of an illusive island call Topazios (meaning "to seek"). The island produced topaz stones, but the island itself was usually covered with a blanket of dense fog, making it difficult for anyone but the island natives to find the place. If a merchant ship did manage to locate the island, the sailors would find the gleaming gemstones already piled up on the shore, as generous gifts from the natives.[6]

The beauty of topaz is undisputed. In the 19th century, the Portuguese crown of the ruling Braganza family was graced with a magnificent topaz (thought for years to be a diamond) weighing 1680 carats.[7] The error is understandable; topaz comes in a variety of shades including yellow, yellow-brown, honey-yellow, flax, brown, green, blue, light blue, and red—and it even comes in a colorless variety.

EMBLEM OF "FRUIT" AND "GIFTS"

The beauty of the topaz stage in a believer's development is that some of the most magnificent fruit and gifts of the Spirit are revealed in the midst of difficulties. History records many beautiful accounts of martyred Christians who found that place of *"peace… which surpasses all understanding"* (Phil. 4:7). Nero witnessed this phenomenon firsthand as Christian martyrs set ablaze on stakes surrounding the city were heard singing, even as they burned to death.

I can recall in my own life many times and seasons when it was absolutely necessary for me to go through some of the most uncomfortable and even painful experiences in order for the true character of God to be better revealed in my life. The pattern is a recurring one for those who press forward in spiritual maturity.

This principle was clearly illustrated at a time when we found our home suddenly infested with bloodthirsty fleas. Our floors and carpets were full of the hopping pests. As soon as we put a bare foot on the floor, fleas could be seen jumping up to bite us. The children learned to run quickly from their beds to a chair or couch in order to avoid (as much as possible) the masses of fleas waiting to pounce at floor level.

At first I thought I only needed to pray for deliverance and we would be spared from this plague. However, it seemed my prayers were left unanswered. I pleaded, repented, and rebuked with all my might, but nothing changed. My next line of defense was to attempt driving the invaders out with a smorgasbord of sprays, powders, and flea baths (for the dog, of course).

I tried everything short of hiring a professional to eliminate the problem. I sprayed. I sprinkled. I vacuumed every inch of the floor several times daily hoping to kill the fleas, but nothing seemed to work. The highlight of my embarrassment came when a guest sat on our couch. I watched in horror as he aggressively slapped his ankle trying to kill one of the nasty vermin—right in the middle of our conversation.

That was the last straw.

My prayers at the beginning of this ordeal were more complaints than anything else, but somehow in the midst of all the discomfort, the Lord did a quiet work in my heart, breaking down all resistance to His will and His plan. I was finally where He had wanted me to be all along. Basically, I just gave up and laid the trial in the Lord's lap.

"All right," I said. "If You want us to live with fleas to accomplish Your purposes in our lives, I'm willing to accept that." I even went so far as to thank Him for the fleas and for whatever lessons He was teaching us through it all.

Though I don't believe God sent the fleas, I do understand that God will use life's difficulties to teach me valuable lessons. Such was the case that day when I decided to fully yield my circumstances to the Lord.

The day I prayed that prayer was the last day I saw fleas jumping around in the house. The whole attack seemed to vanish just as quickly as it began. We were amazed at how quickly God responded. The rest of the family, I'm sure, was especially grateful that I learned something from that situation before too much time went by. If I hadn't, we might have been plagued for months!

God is so incredibly good! Our little flea trial pales in comparison to the ordeals so many others have suffered, but the principle of this lesson remains. God always has eternal purposes in mind when He places us in less than comfortable situations. It is to His glory when we are able to reveal the fruit of His character in the midst of trials. Those are the times when the true beauty of yielded obedience can be displayed for all to see.

As we mature in the Lord, we'll sometimes find the directives of God running in absolute opposition to everything for which our flesh cries out. The flesh loves comfort and a predictable routine. Our human nature desires recognition and the applause of others. By contrast, the upward call of God may lead to a place of great discomfort to our flesh. However, the joy of serving our Master and the desire for the souls of men keep pushing us forward in obedience.

The beauty of the topaz can remind us of this amazing transformation process as it takes place in our own lives. The empty vessel is filled with His glory and we are able to move in obedience through whatever difficulties He lays before us. The fruit of our lives becomes a precious gem in the eyes of our Lord. It is my prayer that I will eventually come to the place where my personal comfort zone will have absolutely no bearing on my obedience to the call of God.

As we look at the topaz, we are challenged to hear God's voice intelligently and obey His plans completely, regardless of the cost.

REFLECTIONS ON THE ROCK

At the topaz level, we understand that if we stay the course, we will see great victories in the days ahead. God's grace truly is sufficient for us as we continue to choose the way of the cross (see 2 Cor. 12:9).

LET'S PRAY!

Lord Jesus, the sound of Your voice is precious to my ears. The joy that comes from knowing You as a friend keeps increasing upon me; yet my flesh is uncomfortable and wants to complain. Jesus, I ask for more grace to press on in obedience whether or not I get applause from others. I serve You and only desire to please You with my life. Help me in my moments of weakness.

Holy Spirit, I ask that You would try my heart and sift through my thoughts. Am I guarding my meditations and keeping my motivations pure? Am I striving to impress others or am I simply working out of love for my Father? Are there hidden issues that I've yet to yield? (Listen to what He says and make it part of your prayer.)

Forgive me Lord for failing to guard my meditations as I should. I repent of any hidden motives of selfishness or pride that may have slipped in. Forgive me for (name the offense). Lord, I truly want to please You and You alone. Wash me now in the blood of Jesus so that my heart would be pure once again.

In the name of Jesus, I come against you spirits of striving, perform-
ance, and (name any others that apply). I tell you that you have no
place in me! I don't want you any more. I send you to the feet of
Jesus! Go now!

Holy Spirit, I ask You to refresh me with renewed joy and devotion.
Grant me the grace to hear and do only what my Father tells me to
do. Above all, help me to maintain that secret place with my Fa-
ther that I may have all I need to press through every challenge
with joy. In Jesus' name I pray. Amen.

THE LORD'S WORD TO YOU

My dear faithful warrior,

Though birthed in the midst of rejection, your past has been swal-
lowed up in adoption. Your persistence in accepting My corrections
of love has brought you to this place of great accuracy in hearing, re-
leasing My many gifts into your hands. Your faithfulness to give out
what I have given you has caught My attention. The refining
process has brought forth much fruit... and yet I tell you there is
more. Will you pursue My love to discover new facets of who I am?

ENDNOTES

1. Personal interview, July, 2008.

2. Crosswalk, http://biblestudy.crosswalk.com/nybst/default
   .aspx?type=library&contentid=100212&catergory=REF,
   Revelation 21:20 (accessed April 29, 2009).

3. James Strong, *Strong's Exhaustive Concordance* – 5116; Rings
   & Things, http://www.rings-things.com /gemstone/t.htm.

4. *The New Strong's Exhaustive Numbers and Concordance with*
   Expanded Greek-Hebrew Dictionary. CD-ROM. Biblesoft,
   Inc., and International Bible Translators, Inc., s.v. "shama,"
   (OT 8085).

5. International Colored Gemstone Association, http://www
.gemstone.org/gem-by-gem/english/topaz.html, (accessed
May 4, 2009).

6. Ruth V. Wright and Robert L. Chadbourne, *Crystals, Gems &
Minerals of the Bible* (New Canaan, CT: Keats Publishing,
Inc., 1970), 135-136.

7. International Colored Gemstone Association, http://www
.gemstone.org/gem-by-gem/english/topaz.html, (accessed
May 4, 2009).

Chapter Eleven
The Blessing of Full Restoration

... The eighth beryl, the ninth topaz,
the tenth chrysoprase... (Revelation 21:20).

Gemstones had been appearing that night. Arnold, a former missionary, along with everyone else at the home meeting, had their eyes open as they lifted up the name of Jesus. The Spirit of God was responding when, suddenly, Arnold thought he glimpsed some movement out of the corner of his eye.

That was right before something hit Arnold's cheek. Curious, he looked down at the floor and discovered a small diamond-like gemstone near his feet. After further examining his position next to the couch and the wall, he and the other attendees of the home meeting concluded that it would have been impossible for anyone other than an angel to have thrown the gemstone from the direction it had come.[1]

Another time, Arnold, his wife, and some friends had driven to a retreat center to attend a meeting with some other Christians. Arnold and his wife decided to join their hosts in prayer prior to the gathering. While in prayer, the sweet presence of the Lord filled the room. When they opened their eyes, they were amazed to see amethyst, citrine, and diamond-like gemstones scattered all over the floor around them. Arnold and the others experienced great joy that evening as they celebrated God's goodness to them... even before the service had begun![2]

The joy Arnold and the others experienced that night is very similar to the joy one experiences when walking in the prosperous abundance and provision of God. Prosperity does not always come in the form of gemstones; nor is God's provision always supplied in cash. However, whatever form these blessings take, they will always be accompanied by great peace and joy.

THE TENTH STONE IN THE WALL

In the tenth stage in our living wall of salvation, we find the stones of chrysoprase or agate, the latter of which is thought to be associated with the tribe of Asher.[3] The definition of Asher's name seems to fit this time of amazing abundance in the provision of God. His name means "happy, to be straight, to be level, right, to go forward, be honest, prosper."[4] This sounds like the definition of an individual of spiritual maturity in the Kingdom of God!

The prophetic declaration over Asher in Genesis 49:20 describes him as full of bread and yielding royal delights from the throne of God even while on earth! Moses declared Asher as the most blessed of all the sons (see Deut. 33:24). Great favor was upon Asher from both God and man.

In returning to Revelation 21, we find John the revelator standing awestruck at the intense display of future events. While watching, he made careful note of each of the 12 stones in the wall surrounding the New Jerusalem which would make its appearance on earth to fully establish God's Kingdom on Mount Zion.

The tenth stone mentioned as being part of this heavenly wall is chrysoprase (or chrysoprasus), an apple-green variety of chalcedony. Though it is part of the wall, this stone is not mentioned at all in reference to the 12 tribes of Israel. By examining the symbolism of the number *ten,* the definition of *Asher* and the word used for the tenth foundation stone, I believe we may have a match.

Agate is mentioned in the Old Testament. It is also part of this chalcedony family and could very well contain layers of nickel (which causes the apple-green color of pure chrysoprase).

Chrysoprase itself has been recognized as a stone of value from ancient history. Beads made from the stone have been found in Egyptian gravesites dating back to 1500 B.C. Fredrick the Great of Prussia also had a great fondness for the gemstone as he possessed many household objects including two tables of swirling green chrysoprase, each 2 feet by 3 feet. Fredrick also carried about a walking stick with a knob of solid chrysoprase.[5]

Agate is recognized as a stone with a fascinating history. Varying layers of crystalline quartz and occasional translucent bands set among colored stripes have caught the attention of many. One ancient king of Pontus, Mithridates, was so enthralled with agate that he collected between 2,000 and 4,000 bowls created from the stone.[6] Both the Byzantine and Renaissance eras were marked by collections of agate bowls generally owned by royalty.[7] Many European museums, including the Louvre, still have wonderful examples of agate bowls on display.

A Spiritual "Take" on Agate

I find the formation of agate to be very striking, especially as a spiritual application. As I understand it, each agate is formed in a cavity within a host rock such as lava stone. Various minerals flow into the cavity and harden causing agates to form as round nodules with concentric bands like the rings of a tree trunk. The name *agate* is said to come from the place where agates were originally found along the River Achates (now called the River Drillo) in Sicily.[8]

In a spiritual sense, we understand the host rock to symbolize Christ and the cavity in the rock to represent a place provided so each of us can be hidden in Him. The varied formations of these agates speak to me of the uniqueness and great beauty found in the Body of Christ.

Let's examine further some of the connections among the tenth stone, the tribe of Asher, and the numerical significance of *ten.* The original Greek word used for chrysoprase only means "greenish-yellow gem" but also "gold" and "to furnish what is needed."[9,10] The number ten is the number of the law and represents order, government, the Kingdom (with trials and testing) and responsibility. Ten also represents a time of restoration.[11]

By putting all these things together, we can see Asher's blessing lavished upon us as we have found our proper place in the Body of Christ. As restored individuals, we walk in obedience, accomplishing great things in the Kingdom of God. The Lord always furnishes what is needed to accomplish His purposes on earth and our obedience allows us to participate in this process. Walking in proper alignment with our Lord through His new law of love also brings great joy, despite the challenges we face.

The Bible is full of examples of individuals who walked in full restoration, enabling them to flow in the supernatural realm of God's Kingdom, just as naturally as they did in the earthly realm. Jesus, of course, is our prime example as we see Him moved with compassion to the point where He was healing those around Him, casting out demons, performing great miracles, and speaking words of life everywhere He went.

Another biblical example of full restoration can be observed in the life of Philip the evangelist (not to be confused with Philip, one of the original 12 disciples). This man was obviously a second-generation convert first mentioned in Acts 6 as one of the seven famous deacons chosen to help serve the needs of the growing Church. He was described as having a good reputation, full of the Holy Spirit and wisdom (see Acts 6:5).

A demonstration of the complete restoration wrought through Philip's ministry can be seen several chapters later when Philip is found preaching in Samaria with healings and miracles following him. Acts 8:6-8 tells us that multitudes responded to the Good News and that there was *"great joy in that city"* as a result of his ministry (Acts 6:8).

Peter and John were later sent in to follow up with more teaching and ministry in that town.

In Acts 8:26, Philip was sent out by the Lord on another mission in which he was instructed to walk along a desert road leading from Jerusalem. Though the instructions seemed a little strange, Philip knew God had something special in mind. While Philip walked, a chariot passed by him, and he was instructed to run alongside in order to speak with the Ethiopian official riding in the chariot. Once in the chariot, Philip's words pierced the heart of the eunuch. Before long, the man requested they stop at a watering hole along the roadside for him to be baptized. (See Acts 8:27-38.)

No sooner had the eunuch been baptized when Philip was instantly "caught away" by the Spirit of God and deposited in the town of Azotus. We are told that, once there, Philip continued preaching in all the towns until he arrived at Caesarea (see Acts 8:39-40). Little else is known about the other evangelistic feats of this man, but later, we're told that he and his four prophetess daughters resided in Caesarea (see Acts 21:8-9). Paul even made a point of stopping in this town and staying with Philip during one of his missionary journeys.

As a man of restoration, Philip accomplished great feats in the Kingdom of God. Though he started as a deacon, God was able to use this ordinary man for His supernatural purposes. The same applies to each of us. As we grow in our walk of faith, God will use us in amazing ways.

A Taste of the Supernatural

In my own life, I experienced another taste of God's supernatural power flowing through me. Around the age of 19, I was invited to work for a week at a Christian camp as a counselor for a children's program. Another young woman and I were assigned to oversee a group of 10 to 12 young girls. That week we were privileged to minister to those girls after each power-filled service during which the Holy Spirit and His workings were emphasized.

After the service one evening, we returned to our cabin to prepare for bed. One of the young girls came up to us and asked if we would pray for her to receive the baptism of the Holy Spirit. The other counselor and I gladly joined her in prayer and were so blessed to see her being touched by God's power.

Shortly after we finished praying and the girls climbed into their bunks for the night, the other counselor asked if she could briefly talk with me outside the cabin. We stepped outside into the cool night air.

"Do you know what you were saying in there?" she asked me. I was puzzled at her question.

"I don't know exactly," I responded as I had been praying in the Spirit during that time. "Why do you ask?"

"While we were praying, I could hear you, and you were speaking in Japanese."

I was shocked! At that time, I didn't even recall hearing Japanese before. I was a little puzzled about how this blond, blue-eyed Caucasian knew Japanese. Then she explained that her dad was a pilot and had worked for an international airline. Her family had lived in Japan for several years, where she had learned the language.

"What was I saying?"

"You were worshiping God using very formal Japanese that is reserved for addressing royalty," she told me. We were both touched and encouraged as we marveled at the amazing God we serve.

Another time, I can recall an evening prayer meeting where the Spirit of God was doing a quick work in the lives of many young people in attendance. The room was filled with teenagers hungry for more of the Lord. As leaders, several of us were going around the room praying for others; we were amazed to see the Holy Spirit fall on the teenagers nearly as fast as we could lay our hands on them.

Greg, one of my friends from high school, happened to be in our line and was instantly lit up with the power of God and began praying in the

Spirit. Mencho, the girl sitting next to him, was an exchange student from Peru. By the time we laid our hands on her head, she too was praying in the Spirit.

Later that night, we found that God had done something extra special for her, as she had been struggling to understand what was going on. As Greg began praying in the Spirit, Mencho heard him in Spanish. The Holy Spirit Himself explained to Mencho what was going on so that, when we arrived to pray for her, she was able to receive the gift God intended for her to have.

The amazing thing about this was that Greg had never been able to master Spanish in school. In fact, he had flunked out of Spanish class! Yet, God used him to speak clearly to an exchange student desiring a touch from God! Wow! That just boggles my mind when I think about it!

As I understand it, walking in full restoration indicates a special time where needs for the work of the Kingdom are quickly met. Progress is made in establishing God's authority in whatever area we find ourselves. This does not mean there won't be challenges or temporary trials to overcome, but with the solid foundation of the nine previous stages behind us, our confidence in God is not easily shaken.

We know what God has said. We understand the cost and confidently look to the Lord as He abundantly supplies our every need. As we serve, our joy is filled to overflowing and even splashes out upon those around us.

REFLECTIONS ON THE ROCK

As we look at the swirling layers of color found in the beautiful agates, we can be reminded of the many amazing ways God surprises us in furnishing whatever we need so that our restored lives can touch others. We don't have to understand it. We just get to rest in our designated positions in the Body of Christ and watch God do His amazing works through us. What a privilege it is to serve the God of all creation!

The picture of the agate is appropriate for this beautiful stage of supernatural restoration! Once we have found our proper place in the Body of Christ and are nestled into our carefully formed niche within the Rock, our true beauty is revealed. All the tests and trials of the past begin to make sense as our love is refined and God's grace is able to flow through us easily.

LET'S PRAY!

Let's ask that God would keep us wise and alert to any schemes of the enemy designed to bring us down through subtle means!

Lord Jesus, we ask that You would complete all that You have started in us. Your Word says to watch and pray, so we ask now that You would strengthen our spiritual senses to be aware of all that is around us. Help us to guard the gifts of humility and repentance that we might be able to quickly agree with the Holy Spirit when He highlights sin or weaknesses in our lives. Let us be quick to run to You in repentance, instead of trying to cover our sin. Grant us the courage to cast out whatever needs to be removed and embrace that which needs to be treasured.

Holy Spirit, I ask that You would again search me to see if there are any cracks in my wall of protection. Are there any areas of sin with which I have neglected to deal? (Listen to what He says and then deal with it.)

Forgive me, Lord Jesus for my neglect in the areas of (name the areas of offense). I confess this as sin and ask You to wash me in Your blood that I might be clean before You.

Now in the name of Jesus, I come against you spirits behind (name the offense). You have no place in me any longer. I tell you to go to the feet of Jesus now! Leave me!

Holy Spirit, I ask You to come in and strengthen those areas in me that are weak; refresh me in body, soul, and spirit that I might be able to continue the path set before me. Amen.

THE LORD'S WORD TO YOU

My child of restoration,

You have no idea how I have longed for this stage to become a reality in your life! My heart has waited for this time so I could freely lavish upon you all the hidden treasures held in store for you. You could not contain all I had until now! My joy is upon you as we further cultivate our love and passion for each other. Your strength to stand in My presence has increased. My glory rests upon you as you carry My Word, setting captives free with great signs and wonders following. Your love for Me has been perfected; however, one more test remains. My grace will be sufficient for this final stage. Remember My love!

ENDNOTES

1. Telephone interview, April 2008—confirmed by three other people.

2. Telephone interview, April 2008—confirmed by three other people.

3. *John Gill's Exposition of the Bible,* Old Testament—Exodus 28:18. http://biblestudy.crosswalk.com/mybst/default.aspx?type=library&contentid=100212&category=REF.

4. James Strong, *Strong's Exhaustive Concordance,* Hebrew Asher, 836, 833.

5. Ruth V. Wright and Robert L. Chadbourne, *Crystals, Gems & Minerals of the Bible* (New Canaan, CT: Keats Publishing, Inc., 1970), 39; Rings & Things, http://www. rings-things.com/gemstone/c.htm.

6. International Colored Gemstones Association, www.gemstone.org/gem-by-gem/english/agate.html.

7. Ibid.

8. Rings & Things, http://www.rings-things.com/gemstone/a.htm.

9. James Strong, *Strong's Exhaustive Concordance* – Greek #s 5556, 5557, 5530.

10. *The Strong's New Exhaustive Numbers and Concordance with Expanded Greek-Hebrew Dictionary*. CD-ROM. Biblesoft, Inc., and International Bible Translators, Inc., s.v. "ashar," (OT 833).

11. Kevin J. Conner, *Interpreting the Symbols and Types* (Portland, OR: City Bible Publishing, 1992), 54.

Chapter Twelve
The Night Before Victory

JACINTH/AMBER/ZIRCON—GAD'S STONE

*... The tenth chrysoprase, the eleventh **jacinth**,
and the twelfth amethyst*
(Revelation 21:20).

It was Christmas morning 2006 and Terrie heard a thumping noise that awakened her from sleep. She assumed the sound was coming from outside and got up to investigate. Trying not to disturb her husband, Terrie slipped quietly out into the hallway.

It was 3:30 A.M. and everything was dark.

Feeling her way to the front window, Terrie timidly pulled back the curtains just far enough to peer into the darkness outside. Nothing seemed out of order. Relieved, she dropped the curtains and headed back to the bedroom. Suddenly, her toes hit something cold and hard. As she bent over to retrieve the object, her fingers told her that she had received another gift from God. Without even turning on the lights, Terrie dropped to her knees and began to worship the Lord in amazement for all that He was doing.

Eventually, Terrie turned on the lights. She stared in awe at the bright orange-red, 161-carat gemstone she held in her hands. The stone glistened and sparkled even in the room's dim lighting.[1]

On another occasion, Terrie's husband, Glenn, had been watching T.V. in bed. He got up briefly to check on Terrie in the other room and when he returned, he discovered a large pink gemstone sitting in the middle of the bed.

Later, the couple met with a Christian gemologist who volunteered to examine the stone. Unable to fully confirm the identity of the large gemstone, he guessed that it might be a pink sapphire. He told them that if it was, in fact, a pink sapphire, the value of the 161-carat stone alone would exceed that of their house and property combined![2]

While meditating on the many gemstones she and her husband had received from God, Terrie realized that this pink gemstone was special; it was the one that really drove home the truth that the Creator reaches down into our lives and homes to have His way with us. She even began to see our "reality" in a whole new light.

"I've come to believe that there are many heavenly gemstones all around us here on the earth, but with our natural vision, we're not aware of them," she said. "Jesus just has to open our spiritual eyes for us to see them."[3]

The Bible gives us powerful examples of how God is able to open our eyes to see what we couldn't see before. How many times have we read the account of Elisha and his servant in Second Kings 6:16-18? In that passage, God opened the eyes of Elisha's servant so he could see the heavenly armies protecting them. Then Elisha prayed that God would blind the eyes of the Syrian soldiers so they could be led away into Samaria.

In Ephesians 1:17 Paul prays that we would have *"the spirit of wisdom and revelation in the knowledge of Him."* Verse 18 goes on to say: *"the eyes of [our] understanding being enlightened; that [we] may know what is the hope of His calling, what are the riches of the glory of His inheritance in the saints."*

Could these gemstones be a minute part of our inheritance of which we were previously unaware? And what other mysteries might lie before us?

LAYER ELEVEN AND THE TRIBE OF GAD

As we move ahead in our study of the wall, we come to the tribe of Gad and the eleventh layer of the wall referred to in Revelation 21:20 as *jacinth*.

This mystery stone, the number *eleven* and the tribe of Gad all seem to point to a potentially dark time in our progression to full maturity. However, it is clear that our willingness to walk through this stage allows the Spirit of God to put the final polish on our lives in preparation for our entry as the bride of Christ.

The promises prophesied by Jacob to the tribe of Gad in Genesis 49:19 indicate that a troop or army will come against Gad, but he will be declared victorious in the end. Moses states in Deuteronomy 33:20 that all who support Gad will be greatly blessed by God. In spite of the persecution, Gad will remain strong in his authority.

The prior stages of the sanctification process were designed to bring Gad into perfect alignment with God, so during this final testing, he's granted the ability to administer both the justice and judgments of God as directed by the Holy Spirit.

To further understand the mystery stone of jacinth, we learn that *jacinth* refers primarily to a flower of a reddish blue or deep purple, and secondarily to a stone of the same color, according to Easton's *Illustrated Bible Dictionary*.[4] Some believe that jacinth, or hyacinth as we call it today, may refer to a precious stone of that same color. In the book *Gemstones of the World* by Walter Schumann, we find that hyacinth was an old term for yellow, yellow-red, to red-brown zircon, a term that was most likely derived from the Persian language meaning "golden color."[5]

In the Hebrew text of Exodus 28:19, the stone named is *ligure,* thought to be the same stone as the jacinth (hyacinth), according to Schumann.[6] Some Jewish experts believe that ligure may refer to the modern stone of amber, a golden colored fossil resin. [7] A darker variety of amber seems to fit as the eleventh stone John saw in the foundation of the wall surrounding New Jerusalem.

Amber is a fossil resin that, in ancient times, came from extinct coniferous trees; it is usually a yellow or yellow-brown color. The stone is found as round, irregular lumps, grains, or drops. After a heavy storm, amber can be found on beaches or shallow waters surrounding the Baltic Sea as there is a large reserve of amber on the seabed there. Occasionally, extinct species of insects are found encased in samples of amber making this fossil gemstone even more valuable to collectors.

Amber has been used in the making of jewelry and religious objects throughout history. The Greeks called amber *electron* or *sunmade,* perhaps because the stone becomes electrically charged when rubbed with a cloth.[8] In recent years, amber played into the plot of the movie *Jurassic Park.* (Dinosaur DNA was supposedly extracted from a mosquito trapped in the hardened resin.) The popularity of this movie caused a worldwide surge in demand for amber jewelry.[9]

Zircon, one of the oldest known gemstones, has maintained a mysterious history. Even its composition remained unknown until 1789. This stone can range in color from reds, greens, yellows, oranges, and blues, to completely colorless. The colorless variety closely rivals the diamond in brilliance and luster. Widespread trade in amber may have started as early as 9,000 years ago when Scandinavian sailors and traders of the Baltic area carried it all the way through Mediterranean River routes to Crete, the world's marketplace of that day.[10]

In further examining the biblical word *jacinth* we find that, in the Greek, it means "deep blue color."[11] The number eleven indicates incompleteness, disorganization, disintegration, and lawlessness, while the Hebrew root from which the name *Gad* is derived means "to crowd upon, i.e., attack."[12] None of definitions sound very promising. Yet by examining biblical principles, we can gain valuable insight into what amber or other dark stones might represent in our own lives.

APPLICATIONS, YESTERDAY AND TODAY

From a biblical perspective, the golden stone might remind us of the flames of the brightly burning fire needed to transform both gold and silver into their purest state.

The refining process is ongoing in our own lives. It continues to purge us from things that don't belong in the Kingdom of God. The refining process often feels like a walk through *"the valley of the shadow of death"* (Ps. 23:4). Unless we're willing to walk through life's valleys, we will miss out on opportunities to mature in this earthly life.

The apparent darkness of this eleventh stage of development is not something we may desire when we're in earlier stages of growth. Yet internal change occurs throughout the maturing process, as we continue to lay down our lives upon the altar. By the time we've walked through restoration, there is no fear of death. Fear of the unknown is laid aside like an old rag. Confidence in the Lord and in His ability to meet whatever might be ahead soars to an all-time high.

Our only goal by this time is to fulfill whatever God's plan may be. If more souls can be brought into the Kingdom of God by our death, then so be it. If there is more to be accomplished through our lives, we are willing to wait for our rewards.

The amber stage of the Christian life brings us to the place where, whether we live or die makes no difference to us; what matters is that we are serving our King. If He chooses to walk us through the fire unscathed as He did Shadrach, Meshach and Abed-Nego in Daniel chapter 3, so be it. If He desires for us to lay down our lives physically like so many martyrs have done throughout history, that's fine, too.

Paul says it so profoundly in Romans 14:8,

For if we live, we live to the Lord; and if we die, we die to the Lord. Therefore, whether we live or die, we are the Lord's.

To Paul, his own life had no real value to him other than the ability it gave him to complete the race the Lord had destined for him.

Once we arrive at this stage, darkness literally trembles, because we have become God's unstoppable force. Our lives will shake the world no matter what the enemy may throw at us. From this perspective, a martyr's death has just as much impact as a living witness. The Word of God indicates that even the blood of martyrs will bring forth new life in the days to come. Acts 7:55-56 records the fact that Jesus stood to His feet in Heaven during the death of Stephen, the Church's first martyr. We understand that rewards in Heaven are great for those called to enter it in this manner.

A life and death conflict with darkness was inevitable during Jesus' mere 33 years of life on this earth. Just when the enemy thought he had gained the victory, Jesus emerged on the other side of death, resurrected and more glorious than He was in His earthly life. So it is in the sacrifice of a martyr.

The martyr's path reminds me of the process that produces amber. As we learned earlier, amber is nothing more than fossilized resin from prehistoric trees. But the interesting parallel is that the resin came out of the trees as a result of damage or insect intrusion into the bark. Though the world may succeed in bringing about the physical deaths of some believers, great beauty is left behind as a result of their sacrifice.

EACH IN OUR OWN WAY

Though I have not yet suffered to the point of shedding blood, I can recall a time when our team of young adults had an opportunity to die a little to the desires of our flesh. I also remember the miracle that followed our small sacrifice.

While in my early 20s, I joined a ministry group that focused on outreach to the deaf by assisting churches in establishing hearing-impaired ministries in their communities.

A team of us were sent to a church on Long Island, New York, hoping to personally invite all of the deaf in the community to attend sign-interpreted services. When we arrived at the little community church, we had only a small amount of money to fill our van with gas and to feed the seven of us for the several weeks we planned to stay there. The money didn't last long at all and soon we found ourselves out of both food and gas.

Don, the young man who headed up our team, called a meeting and we discussed our situation. After a time of prayer, we decided it wouldn't hurt any of us to fast for a while, so the lack of food was no longer a problem.

Gas for our van was another issue.

We needed the van to visit all of the deaf in the surrounding neighborhoods; after all, that was why we were there! Don decided that we would continue with our plans until we literally ran out of gas. That was all we could do.

The following morning, we all got up and loaded into the van in preparation for a long day of visiting. When he started up the van, we had a quarter of a tank of gas showing on the gauge. Two by two, we were dropped off at the homes of the deaf individuals whose addresses we had. Don then circled the block and came back to pick up each of the teams he had dropped off. We continued this routine all day long while watching our gas tank slowly move to empty.

Amazingly, we didn't run out of gas. We returned to the church tired, but feeling very blessed by the opportunities we'd had to minister to the various deaf individuals we met.

On the second morning we loaded into the van again, wondering how far we could get before we ran out of gas. When Don started up the van, we saw the gas gauge move back up to the quarter-tank mark. Don just assumed that the gas gauge was stuck. Again, we watched the gauge slowly drop down to empty as we made our rounds through yet another neighborhood.

By the third morning, we fully expected the tank to be empty, as it had been when we parked it the night before. However, when Don started up the van, we were all amazed to see the gas gauge return to the one-quarter mark for the third time! We knew we had witnessed the miraculous provision of God! However, the Lord was not finished in amazing us with His goodness.

After completing our third day of visiting, we returned to the church in the evening to minister in music, sign language, and drama as our team was accustomed to doing. Three days of witnessing while fasting had left us a little leaner, but we were determined not to mention our lack of food to anyone in the church.

Right before the service, the pastor came to speak with us, realizing that he had neglected to tell us about the meal arrangements made by the church. There was a nice little restaurant right around the corner; they had agreed to feed all of us three meals a day for as long as we stayed at the church. That night after the service, our fasting came to an end as we rejoiced in the provision of God. He is so incredibly good!

This little illustration might remind each of us that when we come to the end of ourselves, feeling as though we are completely empty of our own resources, God is always there ready to surprise us with new grace and provision for that day. His daily bread is sufficient. His mercies are new every morning.

The honey golden stone of amber may represent fiery tests in this stage that reveal godly character in each of us. At this point, we are able to accept any challenge, whether we live or die according to the plan of God for our lives. We understand that great rewards await those of us who choose to finish the course and complete the race regardless of what we face along the way.

Let's pray that we will join Paul in declaring: *"I have fought the good fight, I have finished the race, I have kept the faith"* (2 Tim. 4:7).

REFLECTIONS ON THE ROCK

After all that we've experienced to this point, trials and fiery ordeals are nothing new. But many things have changed within us. In the amber stage, our hearts have been set to complete the course; it's just a matter of time before we are able to see the finish line in front of us. The enemy may think that when he throws tough times at us, our resolve will waver, but the truth is that any trials at the end of our race only serve as the final polish on a truly magnificent gem in the Kingdom of God.

Our love for the Father is so complete that we can think of nothing other than the great privilege of finally seeing our God face to face. Our foundation sits solidly upon the Rock. Even a time of darkness cannot shake the heart of one who sees the finish line just ahead.

LET'S PRAY!

Lord Jesus, our eyes are upon You, the Author and Finisher of our faith. We understand that in You we have all we need to stand firm even in our darkest hours. You have prepared us for such a time as this, allowing our lights to shine brightly, piercing the darkness with Your love.

Holy Spirit, I ask You to strengthen my resolve to search the depths of my Father's love even while surrounded by darkness. If You see anything in this world that I cling to, I pray that You would show me. Grant me the grace to let everything go that I might attain eternal treasures worth far more than I can even comprehend. (If anything comes to your mind, release it in prayer.)

Lord Jesus, forgive me for loving this life and clinging to (name the issue or distraction) more than You. I want to love You with all that I am; I can only achieve that fully when I release everything else.

In the name of Jesus, I tell all selfish desires of (name the issues involved) to leave me! I don't want you in my life! I send you to the feet of Jesus! Go now!

Holy Spirit, rekindle my love and desire for only God. Stir up passion and renewed strength in my life. Let my light shine brightly even in the darkest of places. In Jesus' name, I pray. Amen.

THE LORD'S WORD TO YOU

Dearest martyr of the faith,

My heart burns with passion for you as I watch your journey through this final polish of your faith. Your willingness to accept the ultimate sacrifice for the cause of Heaven stirs Me. Your heart is fixed upon Me. Your resolve is sure in spite of the circumstances in which you may find yourself. This is the very hour for which I have prepared you and this will be your greatest victory!

All the resources of Heaven are in your hands. Use them as directed by My Spirit and you will see Me work in your midst. Keep your eyes upon Me and watch Me shake the nations through you. Stand strong! Your full reward is at hand!

ENDNOTES

1. Personal interview, March 2008. I saw the stone myself.

2. Personal interview, April 2008—as reported to me.

3. Personal interview, April 2008.

4. M.G. Easton, *Illustrated Bible Dictionary*, 3rd ed. (Harper & Bros., 1903), s.v. "jacinth."

5. Walter Schumann, *Gemstones of the World: Revised Expanded Edition* (New York: Sterling Publishing Co. Inc., 1997; originally published as Edelsteine & Schmuchsteine), 108.

6. Ibid.

7. Jewish Encyclopedia, "Breastplate of the High Priest," http://www.jewishencyclopedia.com/view.jsp?artid=1433&letter=B&search=breastplate%20stones (accessed May 4, 2009).

8. Rings & Things, http://www.rings-things.com/gemstone/a.htm.

9. Ibid.

10. Ruth V. Wright and Robert L. Chadbourne, *Crystals, Gems & Minerals of the Bible* (New Canaan, CT: Keats Publishing, Inc., 1970), 7.

11. James Strong, *Strong's Exhaustive Concordance,* Greek – *huakinthinos* – 5192.

12. The *New Strong's Exhaustive Numbers and Concordance with Expanded Greek-Hebrew Dictionary.* CD-ROM. Biblesoft, Inc., and International Bible Translators, Inc., s.v. "guwd," (OT 1464).

13. To have a martyr's heart does not necessarily mean that each of us is called to literally lay down our lives…the question is if we are willing to do that if so requested by the Lord. When taking a world view on this matter, martyrdom is a very real possibility in many nations around the world. Even Christians ministering on the street or in gang-infested areas must be willing to lay down their lives to fulfill their calling. Martydom really does happen sometimes here in America. To fully mature in the Kingdom of God, I believe each Christian must open himself or herself up to the possibility of this type of choice, especially if persecution increases in the last days as the Bible seems to indicate.

Chapter Thirteen
His Dream Becomes a Reality

AMETHYST—ISSACHAR'S STONE

And you shall put settings of stones in it,
four rows of stones: the first row shall be
a sardius, a topaz, and an emerald;
this shall be the first row; the second row
shall be a turquoise, a sapphire, and
a diamond; the third row, a jacinth, an agate,
*and an **amethyst**; and the fourth row,*
a beryl, an onyx and a jasper... (Exodus 28:17-20).

Small, perfectly-cut diamond-like gemstones were appearing in homes all over the Redding, California, area. In one account, when one of the gemstones was dropped on the carpet by mistake, it appeared to have grown in its size. Meanwhile in the Spokane, Washington, area, Arnold reported carefully counting 18 gemstones in his friend's hand suddenly become 19 when they recounted them a second time. On another occasion, Carol described how she and a friend were carefully gathering up gemstones from the carpet where they had appeared, but each time they cleared a section, they would look back and more gemstones had appeared!

In the Puget Sound region of Washington, Leola reported that the small collection of gemstones she had found in her home and at several different services throughout 2008 appeared to be increasing in size.[1]

At a small church in Colville, Washington, it was reported that, even as the preacher stood in the front of the sanctuary, several eyewitnesses saw gemstones appearing mid-air before dropping to the floor. An estimated 200 gemstones, some of which were amethysts, were collected in one morning service.[2]

However, the highlight for all those in attendance that morning involved a resolute skeptic who observed all that had occurred. By the end of the service, he was compelled by the Spirit of God to come forward and surrender his life to Jesus!

ISSACHAR'S REST

In light of the miraculous appearances of heavenly gemstones including an abundance of amethysts both large and small, it is worthwhile to examine the twelfth stone; it is the final layer in the magnificent wall which depicts the many facets of salvation.

The prophetic promises given to Issachar seem to match perfectly with this purple stone of royalty. Genesis 49:14-15 quotes Jacob as saying that Issachar is like a strong donkey who has successfully carried his burdens and is currently at rest in his stall. The land surrounding him was described as "pleasant." Issachar was viewed as a man of submission, working alongside others who are equally submitted.

I believe this is a beautiful picture of Heaven and the rewards that await us there. The word *rest* used in this passage indicates a matrimony or peaceful home;[3] obviously our marriage to the Lamb has already occurred. All that was planted during our sojourn on earth has reaped a rich harvest of eternal rewards. According to Paul the harvest will astound us:

> *Eye has not seen, nor ear heard, nor have entered into the heart of man the things which God has prepared for those who love Him* (1 Corinthians 2:9).

In looking at the amethyst as the ninth stone on the breastplate and at Issachar, the ninth son of Jacob we can imagine its vibrant purple hue of royalty glistening on the high priest's breastplate.[4] Each of the 12 stones was set in gold and inscribed with the name of one of the 12 tribes (see Exod. 28:17-21). Aaron, the brother of Moses, wore this breastplate over his heart as a vivid reminder that Israel was always on God's heart.

Today, those of us who have been adopted into the family of God are heavy on His heart. His thoughts and Jesus' prayers of intercession are always going up on our behalf while the Holy Spirit washes us daily with the love of the Father (see Heb. 7:25). Each of us is viewed as a precious jewel before Him even while the Lord is working diligently to cause us to truly shine with His character and His glory.

STRENGTH AND THE STONE

Amethyst, the twelfth stone in the foundation of the wall has been considered a significant gem stone throughout all of history. A stone often used in jewelry created for royalty, amethyst was known as a personal favorite of Catherine the Great.[5] Some rare amethysts were used to decorate the British Crown Jewels. Others set in rings were worn by cardinals, bishops, and priests within the Catholic Church during the Middle Ages; they served as symbols of piety and celibacy.[6]

Skilled artists of early history often carved beautiful goblets from amethyst crystals, some with quite elaborate designs. Amethyst was also sculpted into vases, charms, intaglios, and miniatures by both Egyptian and Roman artisans.[7]

The Hebrew word and root for "amethyst" mean "dream stone," "to bind firmly, to make plump," "to be in good liking" and "recover."[8] The Greek word *amethustos* provides an indication that the stone was somehow "supposed to prevent intoxication."[9] Apparently it was noted that, on festive occasions, noblemen who had more than enough to drink would be served cheap wine or water in amethyst goblets. The glowing purple of the stone created the illusion of good wine inside; the intoxicated noblemen had no idea of the change.[10]

In trying to understand the spiritual significance of amethyst's use in preventing intoxication, I recalled various Old and New Testament accounts of people unable to stand within the glory cloud of God described in First Kings 8:10-11 As I understand it, the amethyst may represent a level of strengthening where we are granted the ability to stand when the presence of God overshadows us.

The name *Issachar* means, among other things, "he will bring a reward," "to lift," and "payment of contract."[11] The number twelve itself represents divine government and apostolic fullness according to Kevin Conner's book *Interpreting the Symbols and Types.*[12] With the amethyst's assignment as the twelfth stone in Revelation's gemstone wall, we can see this representing the fullness of God's divine government with apostolic offices in place. One might be tempted to think of this level as impossible within the realms of this world. Yet, the Bible clearly tells us that the day will come when Jesus returns to the earth and reigns as the King in the New Jerusalem, sitting atop Mount Zion as He originally intended.

What a day to behold!

On a more personal level, I see the amethyst as a reminder of the future. I'm promised that if I pursue the Lord with all my heart, soul, mind, and strength (see Mark 12:30 and Luke 10:27), He will allow me to find Him and experience all His fullness to the level I can handle (see Prov. 8:17). As I dig deep in my pursuit of knowing the Lord (see Matt. 5:6), the day will come when I will be able to stand in His power and grace as a child of the King, administering all He desires to pour out upon others. To me, that's an exciting goal.

Throughout the Bible, we see numerous examples of the number *12* and its accompanying meanings. In addition to the 12 tribes of Israel and the 12 apostles, we find 12 wells of water surrounded by 70 palm trees in the town of Elim (see Exod. 15:27). The name *Elim* denotes, in part, a place of strength, though it is interesting that Elim was also the place the Israelites went after leaving Marah, the place of the bitter waters where Moses brought healing (see Exod. 15:23-27).

In applying spiritual significance to all of this, we see that as we are healed of all our sinful ways, we can become a place of both strength and wells of refreshing for others. Palm trees symbolize uprightness and fruitfulness, so when we see 70 of them surrounding the 12 wells, we can see an Old Testament picture reminding us of the 70 disciples who were sent out from Jesus and the 12 apostles to the surrounding cities carrying the good news with them. We're told in Luke 10:17 that after Jesus appointed the 70 to go out, they later returned with joy reporting the victories they had witnessed.

THE INSPIRATION OF VICTORY

In my own life, I've been privileged to see spiritual victories that have inspired me to continue my personal pursuit of the character of God. One such victory occurred when I felt an impulse to have my nails done at a particular nail salon in our hometown.

For months, I made regular visits to the salon so I could visit and share Jesus with Michelle, a Vietnamese woman who worked there. Before each visit to this place of business (which was filled with Buddha statues, incense, and daily fruit offerings) I would bind the devil of deception and declare that the Kingdom of God was loosed in the salon. Every time I came in, I made it a point to tell Michelle about a miracle or anything else God was doing in my life. As she worked on my nails, she would listen and smile politely; but she never really responded to what I was sharing.

Finally the day came when Michelle complained of arthritic pain which made her job a painful ordeal. I asked if I could pray for her and she agreed. We stood together near the entrance and I spoke healing over her fingers in the name of Jesus. When we finished praying, I told her to continue thanking Jesus for the healing every time she thought about her hands.

Two weeks later, I stopped by the salon to see how Michelle was doing. Excitedly, she told me that her hands had been healed and they no longer hurt. Even her husband, who was also Vietnamese, had noticed the change and asked her what had happened.

"One of my customers prayed for me," Michelle explained, "and now they don't hurt anymore." Both of them watched over the following weeks as the fingers slowly straightened out and the swelling in her knuckles diminished.

When I finally came back to have my nails done again, she told me that she wanted to have that same power to pray for people so they also could be healed. Patiently, I explained that this power was not mine to give, but a gift from Jesus. Over the next hour or so, she listened carefully as I explained the story of Jesus and His resurrection.

"Buddha is dead and unable to do anything for anyone," I said. "His body decayed in the ground just like all humans. Only Jesus has come back from the dead and is still alive today."

She agreed that praying to Buddha had been pointless. She was miserable. By the end of the appointment, my friend was ready to pray and surrendered her life to Jesus. Several weeks later, she found a Vietnamese Christian church in her area and ended up bringing her entire family to Jesus.

A month or so later, I found myself listening to the owner of the salon, who was describing how miserable her life had been lately. Michelle smiled as I took the opportunity to share Jesus with this woman. With Michelle's encouragement, the salon owner also abandoned Buddhism and came to know Jesus as her Savior.

The little nail salon was changed that day. No longer was it a den of deception, but the light of truth had burst in, giving hope to the captives and eventually setting them free. It was so thrilling to be an extension of the Kingdom of God—even in a nail salon. This is what God wants to do through my life. This is what the Lord desires to do through each one of us on a daily basis.

Dr. Martin Luther King Jr. once gave his now famous speech entitled "I Have a Dream," in which he declared in faith that the day would come when races would be viewed as equals enabling them to walk together in peace. In the Bible, *dream* means to have a vision in the night. Dr. Martin Luther King Jr. had a vision of what it might be like for people of all races to love each other as God intended. Though the darkness of injustice surrounded him, he dreamed of a different future.

REFLECTIONS ON THE ROCK

Amethyst is God's dream stone. God has a dream for each of us. His vision is to see us fully walking as His children, filled up and overflowing with love and compassion for those around us. True compassion combined with the power of God grants us the ability to not only make a difference in our own lives, but in the lives of others.

Without the power of God backing up what we say about Jesus, our words won't have the same impact on lives around us. Acts 4:33 says, *"And with great power the apostles gave witness to the resurrection of the Lord Jesus. And great grace was upon them all."* Acts 5:12 says, *"And through the hands of the apostles many signs and wonders were done among the people...."*

Jesus Himself said:

> ... *he who believes in Me, the works that I do he will do also; and greater works than these he will do, because I go to My Father. And whatever you ask in My name, that I will do, that the Father may be glorified in the Son. If you ask anything in My name, I will do it* (John 14:12-14).

In the same chapter of John, Jesus said that He was sending us a Helper, the Spirit of truth we now know as the Holy Spirit. It's the Holy Spirit who is challenging each of us to yield to God, level by level, submitting to the trials and training necessary for us to begin living as our heavenly Father intends.

Yes, our Father has a dream and each of us is called to live that dream. It is our destiny to make His dreams a reality. As friends of God, we can live today in the reality of tomorrow's perfect world where Jesus is seated on the throne of earth and all is in order as it should be.

By dying to our "rights," and letting go of our "injustices," we are allowing the King of kings to have His way in our lives. Motivated only by love, the Body of Christ will move as one in unity with the King to shower this world with all the many gifts He desires to give...gifts of healing, gifts of mercy, gifts of languages, gifts of all kinds of signs and wonders to draw this dying world to Himself. This is the dream of our Father.

The royal purples of amethyst can serve as our reminder of what we can be in Christ as we dream of the day we can join Abraham, Moses, Elijah, and Paul the apostle before the throne of God declaring that we have run our course; we have finished the race; we have fulfilled our destiny on earth! (See Second Timothy 4:7.)

LET'S PRAY

Lord, I know Your dream for me is so much bigger than I can even imagine. In so many ways, it seems easier to just accept the world's image of who I am and never step out to discover who You say I am. I know I am the one who puts limitations on You by allowing my logic to determine my level of faith. I often make the everyday choices to go the "easy" way in life rather than believing what you say about me.

Right here and right now, I want to choose Your dreams over my dreams; Your thoughts over my thoughts; Your ways over my ways. I know that in making this choice, I become fully dependent upon You to fulfill all that You desire for me. I can do nothing on my own to make this happen, other than believing and stepping out in obedience.

I declare that You are able to do all that is written in Your Word and even more in my life! I cast down every vain thought that says I am unworthy or incapable of fulfilling Your call to this amethyst stage of my maturity. By Your grace, You have made me worthy. By Your grace, You have made me capable.

I thank You for calling me onward and upward in my pursuits of knowing You and loving You to my fullest extent. May Your will be done, may Your kingdom come into my heart and my life this day. Amen!

The Lord's Word to You

My child, My overcomer, My bride

You have found your home in Me! The weariness of the battle will soon be left behind as you realize all I have prepared for you. Your rest and reward await you. Your beauty as you emerge from My refining fires is breathtaking for Me to behold. This is the day I have been anticipating from the first moment of your conception!

Come My bride, for all is ready!

ENDNOTES

1. Personal interview, February 2009.

2. Phone interview, April 2008, confirmed by two other people.

3. *The New Strong's Exhaustive Numbers and Concordance with Expanded Greek-Hebrew Dictionary*. CD-ROM. Biblesoft, Inc., and International Bible Translators, Inc., s.v. "menuwchah," (OT 4496).

4. Crosswalk, http://biblestudy.crosswalk.com/mybst/default .aspx?type=library&contentid=100212&category=REF (accessed May 4, 2009).

5. International Colored Gemstone Association, "The Amethyst," http://www.gemstone.org/gem-by-gem/english/amethyst .html.

6. Jewelry Supplier, "Amethyst's Role in History, Culture and Religion," http://www.jewelrysupplier.com/2_amethyst/ amethyst_history.htm (accessed May 4, 2009).

7. Ruth V. Wright and Robert L. Chadbourne, *Crystals, Gems &
   Minerals of the Bible* (New Canaan, CT: Keats Publishing,
   Inc., 1970), 9.

8. *The New Strong's Exhaustive Numbers and Concordance with
   Expanded Greek-Hebrew Dictionary.* CD-ROM. Biblesoft, Inc.,
   and International Bible Translators, Inc., s.v. "achlamah," (OT
   306) and s.v. "chalam" (OT 2492).

9. Ibid., s.v. "amethustos," (NT 271).

10. Ruth V. Wright and Robert L. Chadbourne, *Crystals, Gems &
    Minerals of the Bible* (New Canaan, CT: Keats Publishing,
    Inc., 1970), p. 9.

11. *The New Strong's Exhaustive Numbers and Concordance with
    Expanded Greek-Hebrew Dictionary.* CD-ROM. Biblesoft, Inc.,
    and International Bible Translators, Inc., s.v. "Yissakar" (OT
    3485), and s.v. "nasa" (OT 5375), and s.v. "sakar" (OT 7939).

12. Kevin Conner, *Interpreting the Symbols and Types,* City Christian
    Publishing 2nd edition (October 22, 2007) Portland, OR.

Chapter Fourteen

The Bride Adorned

I n Coeur d'Alene, Idaho, Terry walked down the church aisle past a friend. His brisk gait abruptly ended as if yanked on the back of his neck by an unseen cord. Making a rapid change in direction, Terry spun around and returned to his friend.

"What are you thinking about?" he inquired. Surprised by Terry's question, Carol knew the Holy Spirit was speaking, so she opened her heart to share her newest passions for the Kingdom of God, the things she had been meditating on just prior to his question.

As they discussed strategies of the Kingdom, Terry suddenly decided to pull out a large pink gemstone from his pocket. This was one of 40 stones which had appeared at his home over a span of several years. For some unknown reason, he had been prompted to bring it with him to church that day. After briefly admiring the stone's beauty, the two continued their discussion.

Glancing down at the stone momentarily, something caught Terry's attention and forced him to take a second look. The center of the gemstone seemed to come alive as they spoke of God's Kingdom. Calling Carol's attention to the stone, the two watched the swirling colors before them. Soon Carol's husband and several others joined them as they all witnessed the spectacular "light show" emanating from the stone.

"The stone seemed to come alive with all kinds of lights and the glory of God," Carol reported. "The lights appeared to be dancing inside the stone!" The group stood in awe for quite a while watching this amazing demonstration of God's living glory.[1]

WHAT IS GOD SAYING?

As we've considered stories of God's glory, some of which were demonstrated by heavenly gemstones, the questions become: *Why is God dusting the earth with heavenly stones? Why gemstones? Why does He choose specific locations and certain individuals as recipients of these heavenly treasures? And why now?*

We have spent the majority of this book examining what 12 of these gemstones might represent. Now we should consider some possible purposes in these gemstone manifestations.

Isaiah 61:10 says:

I will greatly rejoice in the Lord, My soul shall be joyful in my God; for He has clothed me with the garments of salvation, He has covered me with the robe of righteousness, as a bridegroom decks himself with ornaments, and as a bride adorns herself with her jewels.

This writer has witnessed and interviewed recipients of literally hundreds of unexplained gemstone "experiences" involving stones of varying sizes and shapes. Some recipients were business people and housewives, while others were pastors, evangelists, and former missionaries. All were passionate lovers of Jesus. I recorded many stories of eyewitnesses and many of their testimonies were confirmed by others reporting the same phenomena.

So what message could these gemstones be bringing?

Could it possibly be that these heavenly gemstones were sent as a wake-up call to the Bride? Perhaps they were given to the Bride of Christ as an indication that it is time to "grow up" spiritually so she can begin adorning herself with the true treasures of Heaven. As the

Lamb's wedding approaches, God's eternal promise still stands…that He will prepare the Bride without spot or wrinkle (see Eph. 5:27).

Ephesians 5:26-27 tells us that by the washing of His Word, the Lord will prepare us. He Himself will cause us to stand before Him holy and without blemish; but it's up to us to embrace His preparation process. We must discard our rags of self-righteousness and pride, exchanging them for His garments of salvation.

Each time we willingly make that exchange, I believe He builds another of his beautiful gemstone layers adding to our individual walls of salvation. As this exchange takes place, we notice that the walls of protection around us increase in height. We gradually become further enclosed by this amazing wall, wrapped in His love and protection.

Though I have no scriptural backing for this, I have often meditated on the thought that the crowns spoken of in the Book of Revelation might possibly be embedded with some of these stones as we successfully overcome each test in this life. What an awesome treasure to be able to cast down before the throne of God in demonstration of our great love and desire for the Father!

The longer I've observed this phenomena, the more it appears as if the gemstones seem to come in phases or seasons where the stones seem to change in type, shapes, and colors, like the shifting tides of the ocean. Some people only received gemstones during a particular season in their lives, while others continue receiving gemstones on a regular basis. First Corinthians 12:11 might shed some light on why this is. It says:

"But one and the same spirit works all these things, distributing to each one individually as He wills."

Later in verses 29-30, Paul writes:

Are all apostles? Are all prophets? Are all teachers? Are all workers of miracles? Do all have gifts of healings? Do all speak with tongues? Do all interpret?

And may I add, *"Are all recipients of heavenly gemstones?"* Of course, not! God is and always has been the One to pass out His gifts as He chooses; however, the message of the gemstones is a universal message for us all.

If we look at the next verse in this passage, we see Paul encouraging us to look beyond the His methods of gift distribution. (See First Corinthians 12:31.) Our focus is to be on our personal growth and maturity in the Kingdom.

"But earnestly desire the best gifts" (1 Cor. 12:31).

To discover what "best gifts" Paul is referring to, we only have to continue through chapter 13. Paul summarizes this whole chapter by describing the greatest gifts for us:

"And now abide faith, hope, love, these three; but the greatest of these is love" (1 Cor. 13:13).

Paul shows us that all the gifts of God are amazing, but the ultimate gift salvation brings to us is a transformed character that literally bursts at the seams with an overflow of faith, hope, and love actively functioning in every area. If we have faith, we can speak to a storm, a broken limb, or arthritic hands, and they will be impacted by our faith. If we have hope, we are not overwhelmed by "giant circumstances" we face. If we walk in love and compassion for those around us, God can freely distribute His gifts to them through us!

Continuing in First Corinthians, we find Paul gives us specific instructions for our bridal preparations. (See First Corinthians 14:1.)

"Pursue love and desire spiritual gifts, but especially that you may prophesy."

This verse has been particularly significant to both my husband and me since reading Bill Johnson's book *Release the Power of Jesus*. This book demonstrates very clearly that to have a transformed mind functioning in agreement with the Kingdom of God, we must learn to first see, hear, or remember the works of Jesus and then to speak or prophesy these things into the lives of people around us.

Bill Johnson says, "*The testimonies of God are key to walking in power because, in unveiling who God is, they teach believers to pursue a relationship with Him more than gifts or answers to prayer. God is longing for them to encounter His incredible love so they will be motivated by passion more than duty. Then He can trust them with His power in unprecedented measure.*"[2]

That is exactly what all of this is all about!

As our character and mind are transformed, our love for God increases with each area we fully yield to Him. Each step of yielding allows more of the power of Jesus to be released through us. We learn to think and speak not only as children in the Kingdom, but now as a mature bride without spot or wrinkle. (See Ephesians 5:27.)

This truly is the adorning of Christ's bride.

Now in considering the types of stones found in homes and churches, some of the most magnificent stones have failed to fit into any identifiable gemstone category—even when examined by gemologists. This may serve to remind us that many more amazing discoveries of God's greatness await us in Heaven. Isaiah 54:11-12 describes some of stones as simply "*colorful gems.*" These gemstones are most likely only a small sampling of what we have yet to see in Heaven!

What of God's selection of people and His choice of locations for the "falling" of these gemstones? Only God has those answers to give. We know from Scripture that the Lord often chooses the most unlikely people to have the most extraordinary experiences. Jesus chose Galilean fishermen and tax collectors to be His disciples. He also chose broken men and women to serve Him, people who were willing to turn their backs on the world's "perks." They gave up prideful "bragging rights" were willing to become seeming "fools" for His Kingdom—all so that they could chase something far more precious than the trappings of this world.

Paul states this so perfectly in First Corinthians 2:1-5:

And I, brethren, when I came to you, did not come with excellence of speech or of wisdom declaring to you the testimony of God. For I determined not to know anything among you except Jesus Christ and Him crucified. I was with you in weakness, in fear, and in much trembling. And my speech and preaching were not with persuasive words of human wisdom, but in the demonstration of the Spirit and of power, that your faith should not be in the wisdom of men, but in the power of God.

I am also reminded of First Corinthians 1:27,29:

But God has chosen the foolish things of the world to put to shame the wise... that no flesh should glory in His presence.

Basically, we find that God is not necessarily searching for the wise or even gifted people of this world. He is looking for humble vessels through which He can pour out demonstrations of His love and power to the world. He is searching for those who *know* it is not their own goodness or excellence that has attracted the Lord to them. It is His free gift of love to them—just as it is His gift of love to those who have witnessed or received these amazing stones.

God does not see people as we see them. He is not impacted at all by outward appearances. Instead, He is drawn to the hearts of those He chooses. Obviously, the Lord knows who can be trusted with these treasures of Heaven... and more of His amazing and varying demonstrations of love will be coming in the future, I'm sure!

So what is God's message of love spoken by these stones?

Revelation 12:11 says it all for us.

... they overcame him [the accuser] by the blood of the Lamb and by the word of their testimony, and they did not love their lives to the death.

Literally, this verse means that by liberally applying the blood of Jesus and His gift of forgiveness to our lives, the natural effects of our sin nature can be removed. This amazing gift frees us up so both our words and thoughts can be consistent with the Kingdom of God. When our words and thoughts are grounded in truth, the testimony or evidence of a totally transformed life begins to flow out of us. We begin to live and move exactly as Jesus did while on earth with His signs and wonders following us.

Our desire and passion for the Father, Jesus, and the Holy Spirit increase in us, causing our love for this world to wane and eventually die out completely. Our hearts have been so altered by the eternal beauty of what we see before us that we honestly can say: *Whether we live or die accomplishing the purposes of God on this earth, it really doesn't matter.*

This is when our Father's eternal dream for us can be fulfilled. Our hearts have been made without spot or wrinkle. Our desire for the Bridegroom is all consuming. This is the amethyst of God's dream for us.

Must we wait until we get to Heaven in order to shine with the glory of God's love all over us? No! Will He still accept us if we die before achieving a fully-restored life? Absolutely! Can we experience the same joys on earth that await us in Heaven? Jesus prayed in Matthew 6:10 that it would be on this earth just as it is in Heaven. If we will choose to die to our flesh, we can experience this! Does the Father desire to see His glory manifested in the lives of countless witnesses still living on this earth? Without a doubt!

THE ROCKS CRY OUT

Whether it is a gemstone falling from Heaven or one found deep in the earth, I know I will never look at another stone the same way again. Every stone is a part of our Creator's handiwork and each one has a message for us. They are witnesses of creation and the great battle that has ensued for the souls of men. They speak of God's mercy and serve as reminders of His eternal promises. Yes, the rocks and stones do cry out! They join with all of creation declaring the love of our Creator—and they cry out for His return as we all should be.

And so we have a choice.

Will we continue in our bridal preparations and allow the Holy Spirit free access to every area of our thought processes conflicting with the truths of Heaven, or will we cling to what is comfortable and familiar in our past experiences? Yes, God is much bigger than we know. God is able to do far more than we can even imagine...but do we live as though we believe that?

The gemstones of Revelation have a story to tell.

These stones speak of a beautiful preparation process the bride of Christ is invited to walk through. They speak of a supernatural peace that allows humans to see beyond their current circumstances and walk in realms on this earth that have been reserved only for those who are not afraid to believe God and His promises.

This wall of gemstones was prepared as a gift for the adorning of the Bride. It is my hope that each of us will embrace both the Giver and whatever gifts He desires to shower upon us in preparation for the Lamb's wedding feast (see Revelation 19:7-9).

What should we pray as we meditate on the message of these 12 gemstones? Let us declare in agreement with the Spirit of God: *Let it be, Lord! Let it be!*

ENDNOTES

1. Telephone interview, March 2008, confirmed by one other person.

2. Bill Johnson, *Release the Power of Jesus* (Shippensburg, PA.: Destiny Image Publishers, 2009).

Epilogue

A short time after completing this book, an invitation came asking me to share about the meaning of the gemstones at a monthly Christian gathering held in a local restaurant. The group's original guest speaker had cancelled and they thought of inviting me.

With only a few days to prepare, I sought the Lord on what specific message He had for this group. During my time of prayer and study, He granted me further insights into the message of these gemstones, even beyond what I had already written in this book. I was eager to deliver His message.

The day finally arrived, and in my excitement, I inadvertently arrived even before my hosts. This gave me plenty of time to walk around the room and pray. Remembering that gemstones had appeared during previous meetings, I checked the floors before the others arrived and found nothing but a dirty carpet in desperate need of a good cleaning.

When my hosts Glenn and Terrie arrived, Terrie and I walked around the room once more checking for any gemstones. There were none, so we proceeded to discuss the plan for the evening. Suddenly, Terrie gasped and I whipped around to look behind me and saw two dazzling diamond-like gemstones on the floor. I ran over and scooped them up!

For the duration of our meal prior to the meeting, I found myself repeatedly jumping up to quickly gather several of the small, single-carat-sized gemstones that appeared randomly on the floor surrounding our table. Even after our meal and throughout our ministry time, gemstones continued to appear. I came home that night with nine new gemstones! The following afternoon, my husband discovered two more gemstones that had appeared on our dining room table!

On a second occasion, while hosting our friends for lunch at our home, my husband and I discovered 51 small diamond-like gemstones at random places around our home. We continued to discover several other stones even after our friends left.

The great beauty and sparkle of these gemstones is amazing, but what is even more amazing is that you can glance at a particular spot and see nothing. Then, in the time it takes to turn your head and look again, gemstones from the Lord can be staring you in the face!

How does the Lord do it? I have no idea. I only know that my faith increases and joy explodes within me each time I discover another of His heavenly gemstones. I love the beauty of these gifts, but more than that, I love the Creator who continues tantalizing His Bride with expressions of His great love.

Maybe, when we finally arrive in Heaven, we all will be able to watch videos of our time on earth and see what fun the angels were having while tossing gemstones at the feet of God's children.

Until that time, I know my job is to grow and increase in the knowledge and love of my God. It is my prayer that you will do the same.

Reference List

Bernardine Fine Art Jewelry, "Gemstones and Birthstones," http://www.bernardine.com/gemstones/.

Bethel Church, http://www.ibethel.org.

Biblesoft, Inc., and International Bible Translators, Inc. (derived from James Strong), *Biblesoft's New Exhaustive Strong's Numbers and Concordance with Expanded Greek-Hebrew Dictionary.* Biblesoft Version 5.

Conner, K.J., 1992. *Interpreting the Symbols and Types.* Portland, OR: City Bible Publishing.

crosswalk.com, http://www.crosswalk.com.

International Colored Gemstone Association, "All About Colored Gemstones," http://www.gemstone.org.

JewelrySupplier.com, http://www.jewelrysupplier.com/.

JewishEncyclopedia.com, http://www.jewishencyclopedia.com.

Johnson, B. 2008. *The Climate for Increasing Faith.*
Sermon given by Bill Johnson at Bethel Church,
Redding, California.

Rings & Things,
http://www.rings-things.com.

Schumann, W. 1997.
Gemstones of the World: Revised Expanded Edition.
New York, NY: Sterling Publishing Co, Inc.

Selah Ministries, "The Gems,"
http://www.carlareed.com/gemstory.htm.

Semiprecious.com,
http://www.semiprecious.com.

SHEM Ministries International,
"Gemstones from Heaven,"
http://www.shem.net.

Strong, J. 2007.
Strong's Exhaustive Concordance of the Bible.
Peabody, MA: Hendrickson Publishers.

The University of Texas at Austin,
"Mineralogy/Lore_and_Mythology"
http://www.utexas.edu.

Wright, R.V. and Chadbourne, R.L. 1970.
Crystals, Gems & Minerals of the Bible.
New Caanan, CT, Keats Publishing, Inc.

For more information, contact:

HEART REFLECTIONS MINISTRIES

www.heartreflectionsministries.com
info@heartreflectionsministries.com

Additional copies of this book and other
book titles from DESTINY IMAGE are
available at your local bookstore.

Call toll-free: 1-800-722-6774.

Send a request for a catalog to:

Destiny Image₍ᵣ₎ Publishers, Inc.

P.O. Box 310
Shippensburg, PA 17257-0310

*"Speaking to the Purposes of God for This
Generation and for the Generations to Come."*

**For a complete list of our titles,
visit us at www.destinyimage.com.**